Project Management Institute

Project Management Implementation as Management Innovation:
A Closer Look

Janice Thomas, PhD, Athabasca University
Stella George, PhD, Athabasca University
Svetlana Cicmil, PhD, University of the West of England

ISBN: 978-1-62825-031-2

Published by: Project Management Institute, Inc.
                  14 Campus Boulevard
                  Newtown Square, Pennsylvania 19073-3299 USA
                  Phone: +610-356-4600
                  Fax: +610-356-4647
                  Email: customercare@pmi.org
                  Internet: www.PMI.org

To inquire about discounts for resale or educational purposes, please contact the PMI Book
Service Center.
          PMI Book Service Center
          P.O. Box 932683, Atlanta, GA 31193-2683 USA
          Phone: 1-866-276-4764 (within the U.S. or Canada) or +1-770-280-4129 (globally)
          Fax: +1-770-280-4113
          Email: info@bookorders.pmi.org

10 9 8 7 6 5 4 3 2 1

Acknowledgements

As with all projects, this book owes a great deal to a great many people. . .

First, there are the companies and individuals who provided data for the original Value study and new data for this study.

Next, there are the researchers on the Value project (all 18 teams and 48 academics) who carefully collected and provided insight to the original Value data that we re-examined for this study.

Without data, researchers are blind.

Next, there are the resources and support for this project and many other research projects provided by the Project Management Institute, The University of the West of England, and Athabasca University.

Without resources and institutional support, researchers are mute.

Finally, every one of us who has lived a project life knows that when the going gets tough, the tough get going. AND that the only reason we can do that is because we are secure in the love and support of our friends and family who we trust to still be there when we finish.

And so we recognize the contributions of Matthew, Andrew, Christopher & Neil (Janice), Oni & Chris (Stella), and Nela, Helena & Steve (Svetlana). Each of us knows how much you give to each of our projects.

Our grateful thanks to you all.

It has been our privilege to work with you on this project.

Janice Thomas, Redwood Meadows, Alberta, Canada
Stella George, West Bragg Creek, Alberta, Canada
Svetlana Cicmil, Bristol, England

Contents

List of Tables and Figures

Chapter 1

Introduction

Society seems to have always had a concept of innovation, in terms of doing or using something new: ironically the idea of "something new" is very old. Humans seem to have an innate need to grow, improve and change the way we work.

Organizations increase their strategic capacity to deliver value by implementing management innovations, which can be defined by the following characteristics (Hamel, 2006; West & Farr, 1990):

- They make intentional changes.
- The change is to organizational structure, management practices and systems, knowledge used for decision-making, and managerial skills.
- They are new to the group or organization being innovated.
- Changes are implemented to improve an organization's ability to function efficiently and effectively.

The literature on management innovation and organizational change highlights the complexity of the phenomenon of innovation. It suggests a whole range of perspectives and interpretations on innovation:

- Management innovation initiatives often do not deliver the expected benefits (Hinings & Greenwood, 1988).
- Whether the innovation has actually been adopted can be difficult to ascertain (Damanpour & Evan, 1984; Damanpour, 1987; Zbaracki, 1998).
- Innovations sometimes are rejected and sometimes they do not actually result in improvement (Abrahamson, 1991).
- The implemented innovations bear little resemblance to those described in management books and academic journals (Hill & Wilkinson, 1995).
- Innovations are sometimes implemented in name only for legitimacy or other non-performance based reasons; the benefits they might or might not yield are of little importance to the organization (DiMaggio & Powell, 1983; Feller, 1981; Zbaracki, 1998).
- Most innovations go through some sort of modification before, during, or after implementation (O'Mahoney, 2007; Rogers, 1995).

Several explicit calls for further research on the process and dynamics of implementation of management innovation have been made recently in organizational literature (Maman, 2009; Dewett, Whittier, & Williams, 2007; Freitas, 2007). However, in order to explore the dynamics of management innovation meaningfully, you need to identify a particular incidence of management innovation to explore in detail.

We assert that efforts to improve organizational project management capabilities are a recent and reasonably common example of management innovation. Many organizations in the recent past have struggled with improving project management through managerial innovation with varying success. To date, three studies have examined project management as a management innovation (Hobbs, Aubrey, & Thuillier, 2008; Martinsuo, Hensman, Arto, & Kujalo, 2006; Thomas & Mullaly, 2008). By examining the implementation of management innovations with similar intent (i.e., specifically to improve project management practice), we address recent calls for more research that examines the dynamics of managerial innovation (Gray, Stensaker, & Jansen, 2010; Langley, Smallman, Tsoukas, & Van de Ven, 2010), and calls for research that generates insight into the practice of project management situated in organizational settings (Blomquist, Hallgren, Nilsson, & Soderholm, 2010).

This study investigates the processes involved in implementing one particular type of management innovation—project management—and how these innovations must evolve and be modified in order to deliver value. We examine lessons learned from the project management implementation journeys undertaken by 48 organizations from around the world. By analyzing and mapping more than 100 project management interventions across a period of up to 30 years, we acquired substantial evidence of what is actually done in practice. For each organization, we identified types of innovation events. Each intervention made by an organization is an innovation event. The series of interventions formed an innovation journey that reflected the dynamics of their managerial innovation, project management. Where needs arose (e.g., from external and internal shake-ups), organizations were capable of radical change; however, all of the organizations we studied ultimately tended toward continuous conservative change.

By examining project management as an example of management innovation, we conducted an empirical investigation of the implementation journeys of organizations seeking to improve this specific management practice. Management innovation literature asserts that innovation drives change within an organization. Drawing from the literature on change (Greenwood & Hinings, 1996; Street & Gallupe, 2009), four types of innovation events (Persistent, Tectonic, Turbulent, Punctuated) are defined by the pace (Continuous or Episodic) and scope (Convergent or Radical) of the change implemented. These events are linked into innovation journeys that together can become quite complex.

Mapping the innovation events, triggers, and benefits revealed in the 48 project management innovation journeys, we identified several classes of simple journey from the possible 16 movements between events defined by dimensions of pace and scope. These movements between events, or simple journeys, described specific components of the implementation processes predominant in our data. We found that some organizations engaged in multiple Continuous Convergent innovation events aimed at polishing and improving a particular project management approach. Other organizations engaged in Continuous improvement efforts that were simultaneously aimed at both Convergent and Radical innovation, seeking to integrate their project management practice across all organizational levels. Another class of organizational innovation journey began with a Convergent Episodic intervention aimed at fixing a problem with a project management approach that was otherwise working for the organization. Another common type of innovation journey was labeled "revolutionary," because it began with impetus from outside the organization and an innovation event that radically repositioned and rethought the practice of project management within the organization. These four common simple innovation journeys depict specific ways organizations embrace project management to balance demands of efficiency and standardization aimed at improving the fit or effectiveness of project management practices, and the evolution of these practices through time.

For organizations that invest in project management over time, these simple journeys often combine into complex journeys. Analysis of 10 complex innovation journeys provided insight into how value is created and destroyed through the selection of innovation events that either support or detract from historical project management trajectories. Deeper understanding of the complexity of project management innovation as it relates to any specific organization depicted in this monograph provides practical insights for those contemplating such a journey. Such understanding also suggests direction for further theoretical and empirical exploration in this field of the dynamics underlying these implementation processes.

Aim of the Study and Rationale

Despite the call from scholars for greater research attention to the process of implementing management innovations (Birkinshaw & Mol, 2006), particularly the process and dynamics of change involved in implementing such innovations (Langley, Smallman, Tsoukas, & Van de Ven, 2010; Dewett, Whittier, & Williams, 2007; Freitas, 2007; Mamman, 2009), there is very little research to date on the reality of management innovations. There is clearly a gap in the organizational literature that deserves future attention with respect to the internal dynamics of implementing innovations, including how the degree and type of changes to particular innovations is impacted by the characteristics of the innovation, the implementing organization, and the external context within which the organization operates (Mamman, 2009). We attempted to address this gap with respect to the internal dynamics of implementing innovations in our investigation of the implementation stage of the innovation process, including the events and action taken to modify either the innovation or the organization, any pilot testing, and the evolution of the innovation to the point where it became a routine fixture of the organization (Damanpour, 1991).

In this study we are interested in the process of implementation of ideas (in particular ideas about the practice of project management) that are considered new to the organization under study. The process of implementation covers the decision around what shall be adopted and the process of adoption, adaptation, and sometimes rejection. It also includes the human dynamics of making an innovation a reality. Although we pay attention to invention and creativity, and their roles around these implementations, they are not our focus.

Our research monograph presents insights and propositions that are a source of "added value" to both the innovation debate and to questions of how project management can be effectively implemented in organizations. We do this by illustrating and interpreting the notion of internal dynamics of continual transition and transformation by means of identifying and analyzing the innovation journeys.

Relevance of Study

Ongoing critique of the writing on organizational innovations has focused on the literature's continued presentation of these initiatives as monoliths in their conception, adoption, and application (O'Mahoney, 2007; Wolfe, 1994), assuming that an organizational innovation is implemented in totality in every instance. According to Buchanan and Badham (1999, p. 164), innovation processes resemble March and Olson's notion of the "garbage can" model of reorganization, which relies on "highly contextual combinations of people, choices, opportunities, problems and solutions" (March & Olson, 1983, p. 286). Recent attention has been given to the role of leadership and the impact of the size of the innovating organization on what is actually implemented (Vaccaro, Jansen, Van Den Bosch, & Volberda, 2010). Recent research suggests that the diffusion of management innovations is influenced as much by the inherent nature of the innovation itself (and its ability to be adapted to new contexts), and the way these ideas infect particular classes of carriers in the environment, as by any beneficial impacts of the innovation (O'Mahoney, 2007). There remains little research on the reality of management innovation implementation (Birkenshaw & Mol, 2006), or the degree and type of effect that can impact the innovation depending on its characteristics, the implementing organization, and the external context within which the organization operates (Mamman, 2009).

At the same time, organizations the world over are investing heavily in project management, which is defined broadly to include program and portfolio management as well as execution-oriented project management. However, research and media reports continue to indicate that projects are not meeting the expectations of key stakeholder groups (see Standish group results, for example) and that most executives do not see project management as a strategic asset (Thomas, Delisle, Jugdev, & Buckle, 2002). Some observers may believe that this is evidence that project management is not effective. Others might argue that what the organizations have invested in and call "project management" is not the *right* project management methodology, or has been modified from its original concept beyond recognition. This leaves organizations to either adopt another variety of project management or turn to some other management fad that comes along, in hopes of finding the silver bullet required for successful projects. Like many management innovations (Total Quality Management, Business Process Re-engineering), project management risks being labeled a "management fad" (Abrahamson, 1991) unless we can identify the processes through which project management is successfully implemented in order to deliver organizational capabilities valued by organizations.

Research Question

In applying a "management innovation" lens to the study of implementing project management, what can we learn about project management implementation and management innovation?

Research Objectives

The objectives of this study are to:

1. Conduct a meaningful analysis and interpretation of the journeys of 48 organizations that are implementing project management innovation.
2. Capture the dynamics of the management innovation journey—its triggers, processes, and outcomes, and their interactions over time and across organizations.
3. Extrapolate from the study of project management implementation efforts to contribute to our understanding of the process and nature of management innovation, and to our knowledge of project management implementation.
4. Identify practical implications for participating organizational members at all levels who are engaging in such an innovation journey. Provide guidance for organizations and project managers on how to effectively implement strategic project management change initiatives by paying attention to issues such as power, learning, sustainability, flexibility, creativity, uncertainty, stabilization, socialization, and identity.

Empirical Evidence

Data for this study was drawn from two sources. The first is a case study database containing information on the project management implementation efforts of 48 organizations. This data set was collected by a large team of researchers working on the *Researching the Value of Project Management* project (Value project—see Thomas

& Mullaly, 2008) between 2006 and 2008. This data set contains: interview data with multiple levels within each organization, narrative descriptions provided by researchers, survey responses, document reviews, photographic and analytical results from the Value project on each case. The second source was a set of interviews conducted in 2011 to update three of these original case studies, and to augment our understanding of the sociopolitical and behavioral components that provide a context for them.

Methods

Our study was designed as a qualitative, comparative case analysis (Eisenhardt, 1989; Eisenhardt & Graebner, 2007) supporting a quasi-experimental design (Grant & Wall, 2009), where individual cases can be seen as naturally occurring series of events that, through rigorous coding and analysis, can yield insights into the innovation journeys of the organizations. We start with the identification of 123 innovation events in the journeys of 48 organizations, and then select 10 complex journeys for further analysis. Each step of these analyses is discussed in detail in Chapter 4.

Monograph Structure

This monograph is comprised of nine chapters, as follows.

Chapter 1: Introduction

This first chapter provides the rationale for this research, an overview of how and why it was conducted, and the structure of the rest of the document.

Chapter 2: Making Sense of Management Innovation and Project Management Implementation

Two literatures provide the basis for this research. We draw from the innovation literature to both position project management implementations as a managerial innovation, and to examine the complex processes of adopting and implementing such innovations. We draw from organizational change literature to operationalize events, journey segments and innovation journeys. This chapter unfolds in two parts. The first part of the chapter explores foundational innovation literature. The second part makes the case for thinking of the implementation of project management as a specific example of management innovation. This chapter sets the conceptual foundation from which we explore innovation and project management implementation.

Chapter 3: Toward an Operational Framework for the Study of Project Management as Management Innovation

This chapter borrows from organizational change literature to operationalize the concept of an innovation journey in order to address the two serious challenges in studying management innovation raised in Chapter 2 (operationalization of the concepts of innovation is difficult, and most studies focus on the decision to inno-vate, or the process of invention, rather than the process of implementing new ideas in practice). Drawing from this literature allows us to identify and classify different types of innovation events and examine the dynamics of how, why, when, and in what ways innovation is implemented over time. This chapter introduces the concepts of "innovation event," "intervention," "simple," and "complex" innovation journeys.

Chapter 4: Empirical Evidence and Methods

The data used in this study and the sample selection decisions in this chapter. At first, all 65 cases from the Value project dataset were evaluated to see if they had enough data on the project management implementation to provide useful in-sight. Forty-eight cases were selected for analysis. The methods section describes each step in our process of analysis, from data preparation to cross-case analysis. Each case was carefully examined and innovation events identified and plotted on a timeline. Further analysis of these 48 innovation journeys allowed us to select 10 more for further study. Three cases were updated through interviews.

Chapter 5: Exploring 48 Innovation Journeys

This chapter provides the initial analysis of the 48 implementation journeys. We explore project management innovation in practice, and the changes in project management implementations across time. Attention is paid to the role of project management associations and standardized knowledge on innovation and attitudes toward uncertainty. We conclude with the selection of 10 cases for further study.

Chapter 6: Ten Complex Innovation Journeys

For each of the 10 cases selected for further study, we returned to the original data set and combed all sources for further details on the nature of the innovation events and the components of their complex journeys. Through a process of triangulation of the results of four researchers over the course of six iterations, and with the help of follow-up interviews, we present detailed narratives discussing influencing factors and the dynamics of the process of innovation for each journey. Interesting insights into dynamics of each journey are highlighted at the end of each narrative.

Chapter 7: Cross-Case Analysis of Complex Journeys

Each of the 10 compound innovation journeys is discussed in relation to the concepts and frameworks of Chapter 2 and 3, and in relation to one another. We explore what a "project management innovation journey" looks like, from its beginning through development up to the point at which our data capture ended, and we consider the role of those involved in the project as well as the impact of the project's context on its innovation journey.

Chapter 8: Conceptual Discussion

In this chapter we return to the theoretical insights we introduced in Chapter 2, and explore the evidence of how these insights helped us to understand the innovation journeys in light of the empirical evidence presented in chapters 5, 6, and 7.

Chapter 9: Conclusions and Possibilities

We conclude with a summary of the contributions (theoretical, practical, and methodological) and limitations of this study, as well as indicating directions for future research. This study makes contributions to the literature of both project management and management innovation. From a practical project management perspective, we also highlight the strategic capability delivered through effective and sustainable organizational project management, and provide guidance for its implementation. This research raises important challenges for future research, and provides methods for how to move the study of management innovation and project management implementation forward.

Chapter 2

Making Sense of Management Innovation and Project Management Implementation

Recognizing the notoriously ambiguous nature of the term *innovation* in the literature is an important starting point for this study. This ambiguity arises from a combination of the term's inherent complexity, and the lack of a single, consistent definition or measure (Adams, Bessant, & Phelps, 2006). The study of innovation is broad, dynamic, and plentiful, involving researchers from social psychology, management innovation and technology, organization theory, and organizational change, to name only a few of the related fields. Unfortunately, there is no consistency in the concepts or definitions used in the study of innovation, and often even if a definition is stated, the means used to operationalize the study are not consistent with the original definition (Quintane, Casselman, Reiche, & Nylund, 2011).

In order to demonstrate how our study avoided the theoretical and methodological inconsistencies of earlier work, we need to accomplish three tasks. In this chapter, we (a) present a diverse body of literature as an introduction to the important streams of thought that must be considered in relation to the subject of innovation, and (b) make a case for viewing the implementation of project management as a relatively common example of one specific type of management innovation. In Chapter 3, we build on what we have drawn from the literature of organizational-change methods to provide an operational framework for our empirical study.

Engaging With the Body of Thought

Before we launch a discussion about the complexity of the innovation process in general, and of the management innovation process in particular, it is helpful to begin by providing some insights into how innovation is understood and conceptualized. In this section, we explore the strongest influences on the field since the early 1990s to capture the thinking within the associated schools of thought.

The Innovation Process

It is useful to start with a generally accepted definition of "innovation," and then to unpack it to consider its constitutive components, the nature of their relationships, and how these components are observed or enacted in practice.

In 1990, West and Farr proposed that innovation in an organizational context is "the *intentional* introduction and application within a job, work team or organization of ideas, processes, products or procedures which are *new to* that *job, work team or organization* and which are designed to *benefit* the job, work team or the organization [emphasis added]" (as cited in West, 2002, p. 357).

For our purposes, then, four important qualifiers of innovation can be identified here:

- Innovation is understood as *intentional*, rather than random, accidental, or purely emergent.
- The substantive idea behind innovation must be *new* to the locality (job, work team, or organization), but does not necessarily need to be absolutely novel (i.e., "new to the world").
- Innovative changes can therefore include systems, policies or structures, administrative (e.g., human resource management, project management) strategies, and/or ideas for new and improved ways of working in everyday practice in a specific organizational setting.
- The notion that benefits from the new ideas and changes—ones that were anticipated and agreed-upon in advance—have driven the innovation, is linked to all of the above, ultimately underpinning the evaluation of innovation (both purpose and outcome). According to West (2002, p. 364), these benefits might include economic benefits (productivity and profit gains), personal growth, increased satisfaction, improved group cohesiveness, and better organizational communication.

There is a notable propensity of researchers to conflate *innovation* with *invention*, or *creativity* with *implementation* (West & Farr, 1990). The "innovative outcome" is generally agreed to be something new (Greve & Taylor, 2000; Gupta, Tesluk, & Taylor, 2007; Obstefeld, 2005; West & Farr, 1990), but the question of "How new?" is contested. The distinction between *creating* an innovation and *adopting* an innovation is also often not clear in the literature (Quintane, Casselman, Reiche, & Nylund, 2011). Some suggest that innovation needs to be "new to the world," a position held most often by researchers who focus on the product of the innovation, or the creation and invention of new ideas; for them, the measures of innovation are often patents or adoption measures. However most would argue, following Schumpeter (1934), that "new to the world" is *invention*, while "new to the setting" is *innovation*. Schumpeter suggested that invention belongs to the realm of ideas, while innovation is the practical implementation of these ideas (as cited in Quintane et al., 2011). Thus the degree of novelty of the innovation is not intrinsic to the idea or outcome, but is linked to the individuals that constitute the setting, and who judge that novelty (Damanpour, 1991; Dougherty, 1992; West & Farr, 1990). Innovation also involves a social component, as individuals need to be convinced to make a decision to use the new idea (Rindova & Petkova, 2007).

Further conceptualizations of innovation in an organizational context have led to modeling it as a process consisting of stages, often termed *initiation, implementation, adaptation,* and *stabilization.*

Two practically distinctive and cognitively different aspects of the innovation process—creativity and implementation of innovation—are frequently acknowledged as inherent to the innovation process. In an attempt to explain their basic differences and the relationship between the two, West took *creativity* to be "the development of ideas'" (normally most evident and intensive in the early stages of innovation processes), while *innovation implementation* is "the application of ideas [. . .] the introduction of new and improved products, services and ways of doing things at work [. . . in practice. . .]" (2002, pp. 356–357).

As in other management fields, models of this kind rarely live up to their suggested neatness, linear unfolding, and delineation when applied to real life. Creativity and implementation of innovation are in a dynamic and permanent interplay with each other over time. A growing body of empirical evidence demonstrates that, in reality, innovation in organizations is a nonlinear process in which creativity does not occur only at the start, to be "done and dusted with," but can appear and reappear over time during innovation implementation due to the complex dynamics of the process (see discussion below on the social and behavioral characteristics of the innovation process, and its link to change and learning in organizations). West (2002) presented arguments by some authors who suggested that not only should we consider the innovation process as nonlinear, but we should also think of it as cyclical. The cyclical nature of innovation reflects the frequent challenge around accomplishing two latter stages of the process—adaptation and stabilization—both in practice and in the effort to sustain the momentum of innovation through diffusion of innovation, routinizing actions, and reproducing conditions for creativity. Therefore, considering the innovation process as cyclical brings academic conceptualizations closer to the experiences in the real world of practice.

Social and Behavioral Aspects

According to West (2002), the innovation process "concerns those behavioral and social processes whereby individuals, groups, or organizations seek to achieve desired changes, or avoid penalties of inaction" (p. 357). His study of impediments and drivers of innovation in groups suggested that group members' knowledge and skill diversity foster innovation. However, interdependence and diversity might also foster conflict.

In this paradoxical situation, successful team innovation will require appropriately governed interdependencies among group members with inherent inconsistent or heterogeneous goals, and with diversity in modes of operation and points of view. West's model of team innovation and integrating group processes (see Figure 2.1) reflected his hypothesis that, besides group knowledge, diversity, and skills, the level of group task characteristics (group autonomy and the task requirements, varied demands, opportunities for social interaction, learning and development) will predict group creativity and innovation implementation (2002, p. 362).

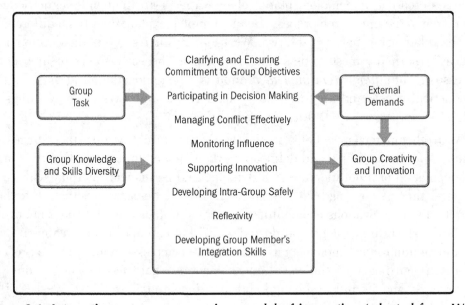

Figure 2-1: Integrating group processes in a model of innovation (adapted from West, 2002, p. 369

Ultimately, according to West, "*either* high levels of task characteristics encouraging innovation *or* high levels of external demands *are necessary* for innovation *implementation* [emphasis added]" (2002, p. 368).

Here, we identify another side of the paradox of innovation: while in many cases innovations in organizations (including management innovations) are initiated and adopted not by internal consensus but due to external pressures and threats on people/groups/organizations at all levels (e.g., organizational climate, support system, market environment, environmental uncertainty or severity, competition, time pressure, psychological threats to face or identity), such external demands often increase rigidity of thinking—thus inhibiting creativity or idea generation (represented graphically by a "loop" of relevant arrows on the right side of Figure 2.1).

However, according to West (2002), the uncertainty created by these pressures also encourages the implementation of creative ideas and acts, and serves as a motivating factor to sustain the effort needed to implement innovation:

> [I]f the environment of teams and organizations is threatening and uncertain, the more likely it is that they will innovate to reduce the uncertainty or threat. Creativity requires an undemanding environment, while implementation requires precisely the opposite (West, 2002, p. 366).

Here a new paradox is identified: uncertainty may be as important to innovation as sustained momentum and routinization, and a systematized innovation process may in fact hamper creativity. Thus, perceived success in dealing with external threats or internal job design might remove the very spark needed for creative endeavor.

The difficulty here is in planning for long-term competitive advantage while providing the time, autonomy and support necessary to creativity. The upshot of this is that it may be possible for innovation to be best viewed as a necessity when situations are unfavorable and a luxury in more favorable times (Thompson & McHugh, 2002, p. 258).

West asserts that group integrating processes involved in innovation need to be understood and governed, to enable cooperation over the entire innovation cycle.

Focusing on Management Innovation

As discussed earlier in the context of innovation in organizations more generally, innovative changes in organizational systems, policies or structures, administrative strategies and/or ideas for new and improved ways of decision-making and working in everyday practice in a specific organizational setting are also considered innovation (Hamel, 2006; West, 2002). In that vein, management innovation or innovation in management practice has been most often defined as the introduction of a new set of management tools, techniques, processes, and managerial skills for the specific goal of improving management practice and an organization's ability to function efficiently and effectively (Adams et al 2006; Birkinshaw, Hamel, & Mol, 2008; Boer & During, 2001; Hamel, 2006). It has been noted that organizations regularly invest in planned organizational change programs aimed at implementing a particular type of management innovation with the intent of improving organizational performance (Burnes, 2004; Caldwell, 2003; Stensaker & Langley, 2010). Recent macro-level research using surveys of innovation and publicly reported performance data indicates management innovation has a positive effect on organizational performance (Birkenshaw & Mol, 2006; Damanpour, Walker, & Avellaneda, 2009).

Marcus (1988) went so far as to suggest that innovations are "ideas, formulas, or programs that the individuals involved perceive as new" (p. 1). Van de Ven (1986) proposed that "as long as the idea is perceived as new to the people involved, it is an 'innovation,' even though it may appear to others to be an imitation or something that exists elsewhere" (p. 2), and Daft (1978) suggested that "the idea can be old with regard to other organizations so long as the idea has not previously been used by the adopting organizations" (p. 5). In this way, imitation may be part of the innovation process, while creativity is about developing "new to the world" knowledge. In our view, both imitation and creativity are likely important contributors to the implementation of innovation in organizations, whether the idea or practice is new to the organization or new to the world.

Beyond the question of innovativeness of changes in management practice, there are serious ongoing discussions of the process of management innovation and the likelihood of receiving benefits from such innovation. The process of adopting management innovation is often described as including three phases: initiation, adoption, and implementation (Damanpour & Schneider, 2006; Rogers, 1995). In order to deliver the valued organizational benefits that are the *raison d'être* for management-initiated innovations, the innovation must be thoroughly implemented (i.e., accepted as a theory in use); as has often been discussed (DiMaggio & Powell, 1983; Feller, 1981; Zbaraki, 1998), it cannot be adopted solely in name for legitimacy or other non-performance-based reasons. Sometimes innovations are rejected, and sometimes innovations do not actually result in improvement (Abrahamson, 1991). Sometimes, despite the failure to achieve the intended outcome, other important and valuable benefits are realized; on the other hand, sometimes the initiative is a costly waste of time (Hinings & Greenwood, 1988). Determining whether the innovation has actually been adopted can also be difficult to ascertain (Damanpour, 1987; Zbaracki, 1998). Perhaps the greatest challenge in understanding management innovations may be the fact that in practice, the innovations bear little resemblance to those described in management books and academic journals (Hill & Wilkinson, 1995).

A management innovation is unlikely to deliver desired results if it does not *fit* with the organization or its strategic or competitive environment (Kimberly & Evanisko, 1981). It is also unlikely to achieve its goals if something else going on in the organization weakens, jeopardizes, or overstates potential benefits (Damanpour, 1987, 1996). Although modification of a managerial innovation can be seen by some as undesirable interference with the holistic nature of the innovation in question, which can destroy the credibility and efficacy of the innovation (Rogers, 1995), we must also recognize that: (a) modification of these managerial innovations is necessary to improve the fit and make the innovation more appropriate for addressing the organization's problems (Hammel & Breen, 2007; Wood & Caldas, 2002); and (b) most management innovations go through some form of modification either before, during, or after implementation to improve their effectiveness and fit with the organization (Rogers, 1995).

It is important to note that innovation in management practice as a research field has raised some of the debates already present in the studies of innovation in organizations more generally, but has also introduced some specific challenges and issues that relate specifically to the management innovation process. The "novelty" dilemma persists in the management field, as do the problems of vagueness and sustainability. Some have suggested that management innovation should only be studied in relation to the development of new-to-the-state-of-the-art management practices (Abrahamson, 1996; Birkinshaw, Hamel, & Mol, 2008; Kimberly and Evanisko, 1981). Such practices might include, for example, the initial development of techniques such as the divisional form, total quality management, activity-based costing, and balanced score cards. Others suggest that the implementation of new-to-the-organization management ideas borrowed from other organizations should also count as legitimate to the study of management innovation (Birkenshaw & Mol, 2006; Walker, Damanpour, & Devece, 2010; Zbaraki, 1998). From this perspective, whether a management innovation is a new development or the adoption of an existing technique likely depends on the timing of the implementation, and may differ both across time and regions, as innovations spread unevenly (Rogers, 1995). What for one organization might be perceived as a totally new innovation may for another simply be an improvement to existing management practices. In alignment with this second set of researchers, we have focused in our study and in this monograph on the adoption of an innovation that, while common to some organizations, is new to many. (In the next major section of this paper we specifically refer to project management as management innovation.)

Deviations From The "Script": Vagueness and Interpretative Flexibility in Implementation

A significant body of evidence from both practice and literature signals that the reality of implementing management innovation is riddled with challenges and unresolved issues. One of the prominent concerns is incompatibility between what is conceptually being recommended or standardized as good practice in literature, consultancy models, or bodies of knowledge, and what is being implemented in the name of a particular management innovation in the specific context of the living present. As mentioned before, management innovations are rarely executed according to standardized definitions—that is, what is implemented rarely resembles the management innovation described in the rhetoric, or even that which was the stated goal of the innovation within the organization. There has been a longstanding discussion in the organizational literature over the rhetoric surrounding certain management innovations (Zbaracki, 1998), and the impact of what some have termed the implementation of management fads and fashions (Abrahamson, 1991, 1996; Noon, Jenkins, & Lucio, 2000). In the latter case, innovations may be implemented for reasons other than improved effectiveness or efficiency (organizational performance improvement). In this situation also, many researchers have found that the rhetoric that describes a particular management innovation is often quite different than the reality of what is implemented (Hackman & Wageman, 1995; Zbaracki, 1998).

It has been acknowledged that, in practice, most innovations go through some degree of modification before, during, or after implementation (O'Mahoney, 2007; Rogers, 1995). Recent discussions of this evolutionary process have examined interpretive variety (Benders & Van Veen, 2003; cf. Green, 2008), pragmatic ambiguity (Giroux, 2006), and translation (Czarniawska-Joerges & Sevon, 1996). Management innovation, like strategic change, is a long-term process, with changes taken both simultaneously and sequentially on multiple fronts and at various levels by actors playing diverse roles in organizations interacting with differing environments (Pettigrew & Whipp, 1993). Implementation of organizational innovations intended to improve strategic performance are recognized as episodic, complex, and in need of being studied holistically—with a view to the configuration of mutually constrained components and their nonlinear relationships (Meyer, Tsui, & Hinings, 1993). Recent research suggests that the diffusion of management innovations is influenced as much by the inherent nature of the innovation itself (and its ability to be adapted to new contexts), and the way these innovation ideas infect particular classes of carriers in the environment, as by any beneficial impacts of the innovation (O'Mahoney, 2007).

The concept of "interpretative flexibility" explains how improvement recipes and prescriptions, which are mobilized for the purpose of promoting change, take on manifestations different from those envisaged. Such vagueness of definition

> [. . .] directly aids diffusion by enabling different storylines to be mobilised in different contexts. Such a diagnosis raises questions about what the "implementation" of these recipes actually means. The relationship between managerial discourse and action is rarely straightforward. (Green, 2008, p. 238)

Management groups within the "receiving" organizations (where a certain improvement is up for adoption) "mobilise these story lines that accord best with their own political agenda" (Green, 2008, p. 239). Thus, interpretative flexibility of management fashions, innovations, and improvement recipes serve the interests of both promoters (innovators or consultants) and users (managers to whom they provide persuasive scripts for change) (Green, 2008).

However, there is little research to date examining the reality of management innovation implementation (Birkenshaw & Mol, 2006), or the degree and type of changes to particular innovations impacted by the characteristics of the innovation, the implementing organization, and the external context within which the organization operates (Mamman, 2009). This study seeks to begin to fill this gap in the innovation literature by examining the reality of the nature of the innovation events involved in a particular type of innovation journey.

Political Dynamics, Power, Behavioral, and Social Aspects

The discussion so far has refocused our attention on the complexity of the management innovation process; that is, its nonlinearity, unpredictability, and paradoxes. Creative ideas and expectations behind the initiation of management innovations suffer from "imperfections" inherent in all attempts to plan for the future—which is inherently unpredictable. As a result, there is uncertainty of predicted outcomes and benefits. The process of interpretation, of an only partially known future by different agents, is unreliable. These processes inevitably involve power and politics. Our short outline above of the deviations from the script, as well as the vagueness and interpretative challenges inherent in innovation, reinforces the importance of looking at management innovation more broadly as part of the political, social, and behavioral milieu of an organizational setting, and in a wider context of organizational development, change, and improvement. As Green (2008) asserted, more attention needs to be given to the complex social processes that shape the diffusion of innovation, particularly when that innovation relates to the introduction of new ways of working or "improvement recipes" (p. 236), such as strategic cost management, quality management, lean, and so forth. The starting point is developing an alternative to the mainstream view of organizations as pluralistic arenas where ideas for improvement are continuously contested, reinterpreted, and enacted, not only by agents but by agencies that are part of the innovation diffusion process (Thompson & McHugh, 2002; O'Mahoney, 2007).

Buchanan and Badham (1999) explained that the major changes in work routines, power bases, and resource availability that are often associated with management innovations require rapid and radical changes in behavior. This requirement for change leads to only partial realization of the initially expected benefits and results, as the affected groups with vested interests and privileges struggle to "translate" the high-level implementation plan to a locally acceptable package. Such local implementation of innovation relies on the contribution, compliance, and cooperation of diverse individuals and groups (West, 2002; see Figure 2.1). However, combinations of inexperience, resistance, and inhibition (fear, demotivation), which are likely to emerge in this process, often severely disrupt implementation (Buchanan & Badham, 1999), and undermine efforts to diffuse and sustain innovation. At that point, the majority of organizations tend to replay or reinvent change programs, which means that an internal dynamics of continual transformation (as professed by organizational learning literature) should be treated as an organic part of management innovation studies. According to Thompson and McHugh (2002), and in addition to the proposed extensions of the management innovation life cycle and its cyclical nature (earlier discussed), there is a need to refocus attention on this particular aspect of the innovation process, as it has been neglected in the literature, with the exception of the literature on creativity. This adds complementary dimensions to West's work on innovation implementation in work groups (2002. See the middle box of Figure 2.1.).

In the mainstream innovation literature, Thompson and McHugh (2002, p. 253) identified a particular rhetorical orientation toward the problems of initial design and development (newness and novelty), and then of implementation and diffusion. In practice, however, "the main priority for management strategy is to create conditions—institutional and cultural—for sustainable innovation through self-generating processes and learning mechanisms in the workplace" (p. 253).

Being a lengthy process, prone to local interpretations and exhausting negotiation, the implementation of management innovation initiatives and associated organizational changes risks losing sustained attention of senior management teams.

> Innovation implementation involves changing the status quo, which implies resistance, conflict, and a requirement for sustained effort [...] to overcome these disincentives to innovate. (West, 2002, p. 366)

Additionally, "Political behavior . . . plays a critical role in translating generic packages into locally workable solutions" (Buchanan & Badham, 1999, p. 160).

As noted by West (2002), the integrating group processes and the level of intra-group safety deserve attention, as they play an important role in enabling innovation by addressing the interests and subcultures of organizational units involved in innovation implementation. This is all context-dependent. However, the integrating group processes (the nature of the interaction among group members) have important mediating effects for the total innovation process. For creativity and innovation implementation to emerge, the context must be demanding—but there must also be strong group integration processes and a high level of intra-group safety (p. 380. Refer to Figure 2.1).

Here we propose that intra-group safety is closely linked to psychological security, which is, according to psychoanalysts, a *sine qua non* element of trust. Consistency in daily interactions is a major source of trust. But how is consistency positioned *vis à vis* innovation? Perhaps it is achieved through such processes as reflective learning, conversational participation, and self-organizing through Complex Responsive Processes of Relating (Cicmil Cooke-Davies, Crawford, & Richardson, 2009). Organizational members become skeptical or resistant to innovation, changes, and strategic initiatives, due at least in part to the inconsistencies that appear in organizational and senior management's policies, public pronouncements, and observed or private behavior. We can note therefore that consistency has a major positive benefit in creating zones of psychological security during times of uncertainty and change. We also acknowledge the importance of free information flow, facilitated by intra-organizational communication, participation, engagement, and culture, and for consistency between small-scale behavior and large-scale strategic pronouncements.

The context of innovative work in organizations is actually in the "interactive effects" among the three organizational domains (Thompson & McHugh, 2002,

p. 254), with their respective distinctive dynamics, tensions, and choices: the labor process, employment relationships, and governance. Therefore, in each specific context/organizational setting, innovation develops its own dynamics, reflecting genuine differences in management requirements, workforce expertise, and interests.

Socialization processes mediate between two key aspects of the innovation process: organizational change and learning. Learning in particular is about socialization of key agents (particularly influential managers) into the "spirit" of the initiative and its objectives and purpose, to ensure their support and commitment. According to Thompson and McHugh, socialization is a process that involves "the construction of subjective identity, in the sense of an individual both becoming a subjective entity and becoming subject to external influence" (2002, p. 243). This involves the psychological processes of learning (including social learning) and identity construction (often involving modification of individual values, expectations, levels of control and influence over one's own activity) in a movement toward the state of "belonging" and psychological security necessary to support innovation adoption.

It is widely argued that effective governing of group processes at work can ultimately be achieved through building a collaborative commitment and transparency into the moral fiber of a task in which participants are involved (e.g., Cicmil & Braddon, 2012). Informal social mechanisms can facilitate the socialization of monitoring, control, and commitment, by creating a common ground—a common rationality negotiated between the individuals and subgroups on the basis of reputation, history of relationships, future opportunities, current formal job descriptions, and other dimensions of the organization that is implementing innovation. This common ground, fragile and in constant flux, yet able to stabilize collaboration and integration at a practical level, encapsulates the notion of trust as defined as mutual understanding "taken to signify and represent a coordinating mechanism based on shared moral values and norms supporting collective cooperation and collaboration within uncertain environments" (Knights, Noble, Vurdubakis, & Willmott, 2001, p. 313).

Several threads from the above discussions of the complexity of the innovation concept, its management manifestations, and the human and political dynamics of its implementation, inform our understanding of the challenges of innovation sustainability: diffusion of innovation, routinizing actions, and reproducing conditions for creativity. Next, we explore why these have become managerial and organizational concerns, and the related challenges.

Sustainability Challenge in Management Innovation

Diffusion, successful or otherwise, is not the end of the story. Where does innovation go from here (Thompson & McHugh, 2002, p. 255)? For the most part, problems in sustaining innovation are related to resistance, abandonment, fading out, or losing out to another "innovation." For example, the previously mentioned socialization processes might not work for incoming managers "wishing to make their own mark on events" (Buchanan & Badham, 1999, p. 164). In these situations, power and influence emerge as preferred vehicles by individuals or sections/groups wishing to press their case in the implementation of the innovation. Buchanan and Badham (1999) asserted that this involves a variety of "persuasive" strategies and behaviors such as enthusing, cajoling, bribing, and threatening the influential stakeholders to support the innovation implementation and change.

In response to the innovation sustainability dilemma, some scholars (e.g., West & Farr, 1990; Anderson & King, 1993, as cited in Thompson & McHugh, 2002) have insisted that the evolutionary, cyclical nature of the innovation process should be more pronounced in our considerations, and they have suggested an extension of the traditional sequence by identifying two additional "final" stages: stabilization and routinization. However, the problem of "What to do when you hit the wall?" remains, despite the proposed final stage. A distinct set of problems with sustaining innovation will always be present.

Sustainability of innovation relies on organizational and individual flexibility—that is, the ability of both individuals and organizations to adapt to new logic brought about by novelty (in*nova*tion), and minimize associated tensions. Transition and transformation (as in the notion of transitional/transformational *leadership*) should be seen, therefore, as an integral part of the innovation process, encompassing emergent, shared meanings and organizational learning. This requirement brings to the fore the issue of an organization's internal dynamics of continual transformation, and the reproduction of conditions for innovation and creativity. Drawing more closely together the notions of innovation, change, and learning may also assist in understanding both an organization's (including its people's) ability to transition and transform, as well as the transformation's range of creativity (as fluid development of ideas) versus their application (implementation).

We will draw on Thompson and McHugh's (2002) framework (Figure 2.2) in developing our conceptual and interpretative framework for studying project management as organizational innovation.

Organizations are complex systems made up of differentiated groups that are focused on specialized functions, and each group has specific interests and value commitments. This differentiation results in a variety of alternate views on the purposes of the organization, how it might be structured, and how actions are evaluated (Greenwood & Hinings, 1996). Different groups in organizations compete for scarce and valued resources, and one of the outcomes of this competition can be dissatisfaction by a group with how its interests are being accommodated. Dissatisfaction based on group interests can be a potent pressure for change, but dissatisfaction alone does not provide direction for change. Somehow this dissatisfaction has to be combined with commitment to attempt a different approach

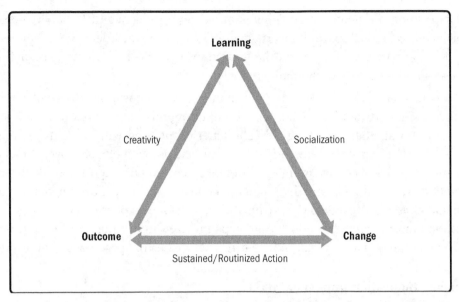

Figure 2-2: Learning, change and innovation (adapted from Thompson & McHugh, 2002, p. 250

that is articulated in the organization's context, and driven either by market or institutional interests. The study of organizational change related to innovation in work processes must therefore pay attention to who is dissatisfied, and from where the pressure for change is coming, as well as to the location from which the alternative models of work arise. People, power relations, and external institutional and market pressures all play a role in motivating change. Paying careful attention to the triggers for innovation will help us to focus on some of these issues.

Sustained diffusion of innovation depends on the organizational *acceptance of the change* associated with the implementation of the "new," and of the adaptive learning that facilitates it. Viewed from this perspective, change is seen as a mediating/linking element between learning and innovation, and as a social process (Thompson & McHugh, 2002, p. 251) that facilitates innovation processes and in particular, aspects of creativity, sustainability, and socialization. *Organizational capacity* for change is not only about an individual's willingness to "be motivated" or to "accept ownership," but has a lot to do with a complex *interplay of identities and interests* (as mentioned in the section on socialization). For example, Boddy and Buchanan (1992), and more recently, Buchanan and Badham (1999), have explored the political and power dimensions of organizational change, and refocused attention on the importance of both agents and agencies involved in sustaining innovation. This approach has been suggested also by Thompson and McHugh (2002), among others. They claimed that the organizational context, history, and power relations that define the structure and culture milieu, within which innovation is happening at the time it is happening, influence three spheres of agency involvement (the labor process, employment relationship, and governance). These, in turn, affect the dynamics of the specific innovation journey on the ground over time—both its triggers, and the processes and outcomes of its implementation.

Organizational change, and indeed management innovation, does not happen through a single revolutionary action, where an organization moves from one state of practice to another in a relatively short period of time with a clear beginning and ending (Hinings & Greenwood, 1987). Rather, practice changes over time, and consists of a series of change events of different types, evolving and emerging through differentiated, localized, and incremental changes, or by diffuse, invisible, and continual changes (Meyerson & Martin, 1987). Thus any exploration of management innovation must explore the events and steps involved in moving toward the desired change as a linked journey that in its entirety describes the processes of innovation.

Managing Innovation Implementation

Another important dimension of innovation is the change agent as related to the innovation implementation. The degree of political power processes that are needed to manage project management implementation varies from one setting to another.

Buchanan and Badham (1999), building on Boddy and Buchanan (1992), have developed a useful conceptualization of the nature of the role and the expertise of the change agent (a person who drives the innovation implementation). They suggested that this person can be described as a *political entrepreneur*—one who is skilled at working the content and control agendas of innovation and change, but also has a mastery of back-staging, that is, of the ownership and legitimization processes of a power political nature that are needed to overcome passivity, disengagement, resistance, and so forth that may be directed toward the initiative they are championing.

Buchanan and Badham (1999) have suggested two dimensions against which the level of political intensity can be understood and made helpful to those in charge of implementing and diffusing innovation (Figure 2.3). These are: (1) the level of resistance to innovation (from "accepted" to "challenged"); and (2) the intensity of associated change (from "marginal" to "critical"). In that respect, research attention also needs to be given to implications for participating organizational members and decision makers in terms of responsibility, accountability, freedom, constraints, control, performance measurement, power asymmetries, and careers in order to enhance the model of group dynamics of innovation (illustrated in Figure 2.1).

A focus on the wider climate and culture for management innovation is a way of emphasizing the collective and contextual nature of action (of "innovators" and other actors). It is also helpful to consider agencies as well as agents in the process of innovation diffusion—that is, to move away from an exclusive focus on specific projects and "change champions" to include the wider cast of characters, as well as durable

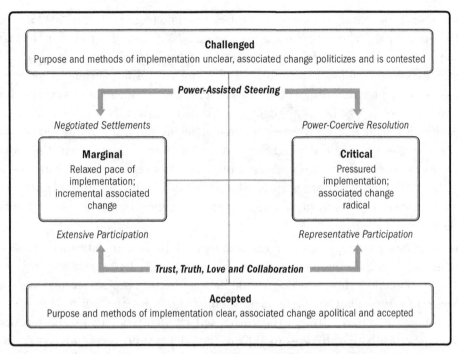

Figure 2-3: Challenges and tactics of driving management innovation and associated organizational change (adapted from Buchanan & Badham, 1999, p. 181

networks and alliances between organizational functions and interests (Buchanan & Badham, 1999; Thomson & McHugh, 2002). The formation and diffusion of the cultural capital by key agents at the beginning (e.g., creating compelling arguments for "reinvention," and the promotion of changes and "new" values) becomes a critical factor. Such a complex nature of innovation implementation means that management attention is difficult to sustain over an extended period of time.

Building a Case for Project Management to be Viewed as Management Innovation

Both management and project management researchers have devoted significant energy to understanding the function of project management within organizations. Few have examined project management from the perspective of what management innovation literature can illuminate, or what we can learn about management innovation from the implementation of project management. It seems clear that, like many management innovations, concepts for project management interventions may originate in published and professed theories, which also explain how these interventions should work, but through the processes and dynamics of implementing change, what becomes project management in practice is quite different. Thus, the implementation of project management provides an ideal venue from which to examine the impact of context on the nature of the management innovation that is ultimately implemented.

Business is becoming increasingly project-oriented (e.g., Pettigrew, 2003; Cicmil & Hodgson, 2006; Thomas, 2006; Andersen, 2008; Cicmil, Hodgson, Lindgren & Packendorff, 2009), with project-based work and project management being adopted in sectors and contexts beyond traditionally project-oriented industries, such as construction, defense, and aerospace. Project management has emerged as a management technology in which many organizations currently invest, which shares characteristics with many other recent management innovations (including Total Quality Management and Balanced Scorecard technologies. Many argue that project management also shares weaknesses with other management innovations—few clear, theoretical underpinnings as to what is actually involved in implementation, when it is more or less likely to succeed in improving organizational project practice, and its value.

In most organizations, the effective launch of project management practices resembles a strategic organizational change initiative, but is rarely recognized or labeled as such. Only three studies to date have addressed project management as a management innovation (Martinsuo, Hensman, Arto, & Kujalo, 2006; Hobbs et al., 2008; Thomas & Mullaly, 2008). Martinsuo et al. (2006) explicitly used institutional and innovation diffusion theories to explore the adoption of project management as a management innovation. Their survey-based research (which included a sample consisting of 111 companies in a variety of industries) identified external pressure and internal complexity as drivers for introducing project-based management. They examined the degree of process change, depth of project-based management adoption, and local success of project-based management introduction, and they suggested that benefits from introducing project-based management included both improvement in project culture and efficiency.

Using a combination of survey and qualitative studies, Hobbs et al. (2008) explored the introduction of project management offices (PMOs) as a management innovation. They concluded that PMOs are a political system that plays an important role in organizations; however, they also found that, as a management innovation, the concept is unstable and still evolving in nature, to the extent that they did not find a discernable pattern of adoption.

Thomas and Mullaly (2008) led a large team of researchers in a comprehensive study exploring why organizations invest in project management, what they invest in, and how the context of each organization influences the nature of both the project management implementation and the outcomes received from this investment. They found that the variety of tools, techniques, and processes implemented by organizations varied substantially in scope from the common project management standards or methods available in the marketplace. The range of implementations varied based on: differences in the strategies employed for training and employee development; different degrees of value placed on, and identity involvement of, project managers;

different degrees of influence, authority, and power acquired by project managers; the approaches that were adopted for introducing project supports groups (such as PMOs); the structure, resources, influence, and focus of these groups on control versus development, and the project management maturity of the organization. They found that the project management maturity of organizations varied considerably, from some whose approaches were very ad hoc and informal, to others whose plans were formally defined and consistently adhered to. Different organizations employed very different strategies, based upon very different reasons and drivers that served as their impetus for innovation.

The Thomas and Mullaly study (2008) showed that there is no "generic" package of philosophies and techniques implemented in the name of project management, but instead there is a wider palette of larger or smaller degree of local "configuration" (pp. 131–135, 172–176, 280–287). The Thomas and Mullaly study also clearly showed the contingent nature of project management implementations (e.g., most-least analysis pp. 87–88, 150–154). Their findings demonstrated that project management implementation is never straightforward but is subject to contestation, contention, resistance, and modification. Paradoxes and disagreements over the "real" nature of project management are apparent, and resolutions are affected by the interests of the departments and hierarchical levels responsible, reflecting the collective and contextual nature of the actions of the innovators and other actors.

A study by Thomas et al. (2002) provides insight into the intentionality and desire for benefits associated with project management implementation. They reported that the major trigger for executives to invest in project management implementations was a crisis in the project management practice within the organization. This supports West's argument that some level of uncertainty and discomfort is an important impetus for conscious innovation (2002). While internal project management departments may chose to improve good practice, executives only seemed to take action when there was a problem to be resolved through intentional action. Action that is triggered by crisis and uncertainty risks losing senior management attention and support over time, due to the reduction of uncertainty or perceived reduction of uncertainty associated with project management implementation initiatives and other changes, which varies at different levels and with different agendas within the organization. As soon as the senior manager's discomfort is alleviated, corporate attention and investment may be directed elsewhere—to the detriment of the project management implementation (Thomas et al., 2002: Hurt & Thomas, 2009). Maintaining executive support over the long term may be a difficult task.

Finally, several recent papers arising out of the large study by Thomas & Mullaly (2008) spoke eloquently to the benefits that organizations seek and receive from project management implementations, and the contextual variables that influence their realization. Andersen and Vaagaasar (2009) and Eskerod and Riis (2009a) both examined the role of both common and unique project management models in delivering value. Hurt and Thomas (2009) and Mengel, Cowan-Sahadath, and Follert (2009) examined the role of leadership, project management champions, and structural supports for project management in delivering value. Cicmil, Dordevic, & Zivanovic (2009) examined the role of cultural heritage in influencing the value received from project management implementations. The role of governance structures in delivering value from project management implementations has been explored by Hurt and Thomas (2009), Lechler and Cohen (2009), and Crawford and Helm (2009). Sustained investment in project management implementations was examined by Hurt and Thomas (2009). The importance of fitting the project management implementation to the needs of the organization was explored in Cooke-Davies, Crawford, and Lechler (2009), and by Zhai, Xin, and Cheng(2009). The interrelationship of context and project management implementation in influencing the value sought and received is examined in Cooke-Davies, Crawford, and Lechler (2009) and Mullaly and Thomas (2009). The complexity and embeddedness of project management implementations described in these studies is the key counterargument to "best practice" initiatives and, more broadly, to the possibility of the existence of generic "best practice."

What these studies reinforce is that, while there is no one way that project management is understood, and no one model that is being adopted when project management is implemented, the people involved in project management implementations believe that the project management activities are intentional efforts to introduce ideas that are new to the locality (job, work team, or organization at large). They believe that the project management implementations require change to organizational systems, policies, or structures for the purpose of generating anticipated benefits that will arise from these new ideas and changes—including economic benefits (productivity and profit gains), personal growth, increased satisfaction, improved group cohesiveness, and better organizational communication among others. Based on this comparison of what we know of project management implementation and the theoretical understanding of innovation presented in the first section of this chapter, we conclude that project management is a popular management practice that many organizations have adopted as an innovation in recent decades.

Chapter Summary

Innovation is a difficult phenomenon to study, for many reasons. The primary challenge is that the term "innovation" encompasses human activity that is driven by varying and often conflicting agendas and interests. For organizational activity to be considered "innovation," it must be intentional, directed toward obtaining perceived benefits, involve ideas that are new to the local participants, and entail change to organizational practices, policies, and structures.

In this study we are interested in "management innovation," which explicitly requires change in individual and group behavior attendant on changes to power and employment relations. Project management implementations meet all four requirements and can therefore be considered management innovations. Exploring the specific management innovations involved in implementing changes to project management practice provides an ideal setting for the exploration of the dynamics of a similar management innovation across many organizations triggered by a desire to improve organizational performance. We seek to understand the social, behavioral, contextual, and performance-related aspects of these innovation journeys.

The next chapter describes how we drew from organizational change and innovation literature to describe the operationalizations that allow us to examine management innovation as a specific form of organizational change, made up of innovation events that are intentionally enacted in an effort to implement new ways of thinking about, practicing, or regulating project management within the target organization. Drawing on this important literature, we pay particular attention to the events involved in the innovation journey and the people, triggers, and contexts that influence the accepted or challenged outcomes of these events. The coding structure for labeling innovation journey structures is both a contribution to the literature and an empirical finding of this study.

Chapter 3

Toward an Operational Framework for the Study of Project Management as Management Innovation

So far we have laid out our conceptual framework by:

- Examining the innovation process, including: differentiating the concepts of creativity/invention and implementation; defining the concept of management innovation; exploring the internal dynamics of continual transformation in the process and outcomes of implementing organizational innovation; and examining its political, power, behavioral, and social aspects.
- Presenting the case for examining the implementation of project management as a specific case of management innovation.

As noted in the last chapter, the innovation literature suggests that learning/change/innovation are closely interwoven and interrelated through the processes of creativity, socialization, and routinization (Thomson & McHugh, 2002). If we understand management innovation to be the introduction of something new to the organization—new ideas, processes, and procedures designed to improve organizational performance in some way (as discussed above)—the implication is that the adoption of these new ideas or procedures requires the organization and the people within it to change existing structures and behaviors. Any effort to implement management innovation is thus informed by theories of organizational change. Clearly a focus on the implementation of innovation in organizations requires us to pay attention to the processes, dynamics, interactions, and nature of how organizations change.

In highlighting the contested nature of innovation, the impact of context, actors, and agency, and the relationships among learning, innovation and change, we recognize the inherent complexity of "innovation in organizations" as a concept, and the challenges faced by previous researchers in studying it. This section specifically outlines how we have operationalized key concepts in order to study their relevance to the internal dynamics of continual transformation, as they relate to the process and outcomes of implementing project management as a form of organizational innovation.

A complete review of the organizational change and change management literature is far beyond the scope of this monograph (see the monograph by Crawford & Helm [2009] on change management and project management). However, we have drawn from a few select strands of this literature to help us operationalize the study of the dynamics of implementing innovation. Doing so has also helped us define which aspects of innovation we are interested in examining in this study, in order to come up with a consistent and meaningful operationalization.

Each of the following sections elaborates on key decisions taken over the course of this project.

Management Innovation as a Change Journey

Innovation is often studied as either a process or the outcome of a process (Van de Ven, 1986; West & Farr, 1990). Studied as a process, "innovation" includes the activities an organization undertakes in order to develop innovations such as: production and emergence (Gupta et al., 2007); discovery and creation (Dosi, 1988); development, problem solving, and implementation (Myers & Marquis, 1969); development and implementation (Van de Ven, 1985); or introduction and application (West & Farr, 1990). Studied as a product or outcome of these processes, "innovation" can be considered to include new ideas (Gupta et al., 2007; Shulze & Hoegl, 2008; West & Farr, 1990); a new combination (Obstefeld, 2005); new solutions (Dosi, 1988; Myers & Marquis, 1969); or new processes, products, or procedures (Greve & Taylor, 2000; Myers & Marquis, 1969). While "innovation" is often defined as activities (Armour & Teece, 1980; Terziovski, 2010) or events (Van de Ven & Polley, 1992), most authors have continued to measure the innovation process as a product of its outcome (Quintane et al., 2011). Following the work of Armour and Teece (1980), Terziovski (2010), and Van de Ven and Polley (1992), our focus in this study is explicitly on the process, activities, and events involved in innovation, and not on the end product produced through this activity.

As the innovation implementation unfolds in each organization, different actors engage in unique change events that in themselves could be studied as distinct changes in practice, each of which moves the organization closer to (or further away from) the point of adoption, routinization, and stabilization of the changes into sustainable, ongoing practice. Each change event in an implementation journey could have its own unique character, and we need a way to characterize each of these events. Most change events are intentional and planned as part of the implementation, while others emerge as a result of the intended or unintended consequence of another event in the journey. It is through a careful study of these events that we can explore the dynamics of the implementation journey and pay attention to the cyclical and iterative nature of some change journeys.

Operationalizing Pace and Scope of Change

Greenwood and Hinings (1996) first proposed scope and pace as two dimensions of organizational change. Organizational change is often characterized as occurring in four fundamentally different modes: Continuous (Weick & Quinn, 1999); Episodic (Nadler & Tushman, 1989); Convergent (Greenwood & Hinings, 1996); or Radical (Romanelli & Tushman, 1994). Plowman et al. (2007) argued that these four modes are differentiated by pace (Continuous to Episodic), scope of change (Convergent to Radical), and the varying theories about why these different modes of change occur. To date, the challenge of understanding the relationships among these forms of change has revolved around the lack of a consistent or comparable way to operationalize what constitutes "Continuous" versus "Episodic" versus "Radical" versus "Contingent," because rates and degrees of change within and between organizations, and different types of change, tend to be very dissimilar. Clearly, the problem of time (historical and relative) and duration becomes important.

Elaborating on Plowman et al. (2007), Street and Gallupe (2009) proposed a method for operationalizing this categorization by analyzing the pace and scope of change. According to this model, the pace of change can be classified as either Continuous (cumulative additions to existing practice) or Episodic (an event in which the change is intended to add something new to practice); while the scope of change can be conceptualized as either Convergent (adding to existing knowledge and frames of reference) or Radical (providing a new frame of reference; this can include an introduction of an established method to new areas of the organization). Radical can also be used to describe emergent change, where the impact of the innovation is different (often greater) than that expected. This two-by-two classification gives rise to four types of organizational change (see Figure 3.1):

- A *Continuous Convergent* change polishes, tweaks or refines existing practices; it is called a Persistent change.
- A *Continuous Radical* change expands upon work done by changing frames of reference, or expanding work to other areas; it is labeled a Turbulent change.
- An *Episodic Convergent* change is intended to make a fix within the bounds of existing ways of working; it is called a Tectonic change.
- An *Episodic Radical* change is a significant change to the way people work, and is often triggered by external events or circumstances; it is labeled a Punctuated change.

Scope	Pace	
	Continuous	**Episodic**
Convergent	PERSISTENT	TECTONIC
	Adaptations occur constantly, and may or may not accumulate, and occur simultaneously across units.	Adaptations occur suddenly and dramatically, interspersed with long periods of continuous change.
	Adaptations to work processes and social practices that are consistent with or support an existing frame or existing organizational template.	Adaptations to work processes and social practices that are consistent with or support an existing frame or existing organizational template.
Radical	TURBULENT	PUNCTUATED
	Adaptations occur constantly may or may not accumulate, and occur simultaneously across units.	Adaptations occur suddenly and dramatically, interspersed with long periods of continuous change.
	Adaptations to work processes, practices, or orientations that become new reference points for the organization and are reinforced by emergent rules that replace existing frames and organizational templates.	Adaptations to work processes, practices, or orientations that become new reference points for the organization and are reinforced by emergent rules that replace existing frames and organizational templates.

Figure 3.1. Four types of organizational change (adapted from Plowman et al., 2007; Street & Gallupe, 2009)

We propose to follow the logic of this matrix toward an operationalizing framework for the study of project management as management innovation. However, this model retains a focus on the entire organizational change, and attempts to describe all elements of the change occurring over considerable time as fitting within one of these quadrants. For our purposes, and congruent with change literature discussed above that recognizes that any planned change initiative is made up of a number of planned and unplanned events that influence the outcome and shape the change journey, we decided to adopt this operationalization of change, but to apply it at the innovation event level, rather than at the whole journey level. Considering each intervention an organization makes an innovation event provides for a fuller investigation of the innovation journey.

Contextualizing and Elaborating the Model

Based on the information we have on each innovation event, we can use the structure of Figure 3.1 as a starting point for "plotting" and analyzing, in greater depth, the project management implementation journeys. This means that we use the approach of Street and Gallupe (2009) to operationalize pace and scope of change (Greenwood & Hinings, 1996; Plowman et al., 2007), but apply it at the innovation event level. "Pace" is identified by comparing the relative durations of continuous versus episodic change over a specified period. "Scope" is operationalized by looking at the number of changes in and across an organization's production system (inputs, process, outputs).

Organizational change that involves only process, practices, or control systems—as one might expect project management to entail—could be defined as "Convergent change," while changes that involve input (strategic orientation) and process (different ways of working) could be considered "Radical change." In project management terms, interventions that simply deal with project management practice would be considered "Convergent changes," while innovations that deal with portfolio, program, or strategic project management affect divisions outside those normally impacted directly by project management, would be considered "Radical change" (see Figure 3.2).

Innovation events are linked into a journey because the outcome of one innovation either triggers—or causes unforeseen outcomes that trigger—the need for another innovation event. Our aim is to describe and understand the dynamics that underlie these innovation journeys, drawing on the concepts summarized in Figure 3.2.

This model allows us to address the question of what kind of innovation we are studying by categorizing individual events into unique innovation journeys, which avoids the necessity for us to dichotomize or typify the entire innovation journey. Conceptually, the preceding discussion has prepared us to examine a high level of uncertainty unfolding over time, evolutionary and cyclical activity, and collective and contextually situated action involved in the internal dynamics of continual transformation in the process and outcomes of implementing project management as organizational (management) innovation.

	Continuous	Episodic
Convergent	Improvement within single division that improves upon or supports existing practices: i.e., revision to templates and tool kits supporting existing PM frame. These are known as PERSISTENT EVENTS	PM improvement that supports existing practices but that are disruptive: i.e., introduction of new automated tool to support PM practice. These are known as TECTONIC EVENTS
Radical	PM improvement aimed at moving PM practices into other divisions and across the organization. Training for non-project managers. These are known as TURBULENT EVENTS	PM improvement that addresses specific perceived weaknesses in existing practice by introducing new practices and rolling this new practice out enterprise wide: i.e., introduction of PM. These are known as PUNCTUATED EVENTS

Figure 3.2. Event matrix: contextualization of pace and scope (adapted from Ploughman et al., 2007; Street & Gallupe, 2009)

Innovation Events and Innovation Journeys

In this section we explain the information we envisage being encapsulated in each innovation event (to be represented by a dot) and journey (to be represented by a set of dots connected by arrows).

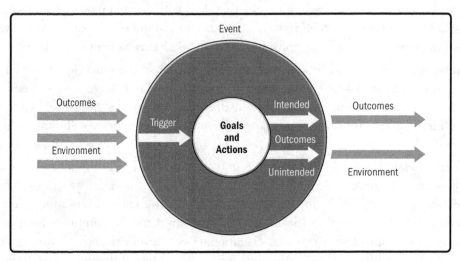

Figure 3.3. Representation of key elements of an innovation event

The Innovation Event

In this research an innovation event is described in terms of the trigger, goal, actions, and outcomes associated with an innovation. The environment of an organization creates continual triggers for change. Time passes while a trigger becomes important enough to be detected, goals are set, action is taken (an intervention) and outcomes are experienced. Each innovation event is seen as a change in practice that could in itself be viewed as an instance of organizational change and characterized in terms of its pace and scope of change (as described in Figure 3.2).

The Innovation Journey

The implementation of any innovation can be viewed as a series of linked innovation events and described as an innovation journey. A simple journey can be depicted as the movement from one innovation event to another, as illustrated in Figure 3.4. A more complex journey links multiple, and often different types, of innovation events together.

Because Street and Gallupe (2009) were interested in describing the entire organizational change effort, they did not explore what it would mean if an organization were to switch in the midst of its Persistent organizational change to a Tectonic or Punctuated change. We, however, were interested in looking at chains of innovation

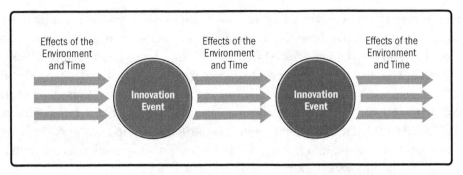

Figure 3.4. Representation of an innovation journey involving two innovation events

events, each involving organizational changes. In this context it is important for us to think about what it means to move from one type of organizational change to another. Examining Figure 3.1 indicates that there are 12 different potential types of simple innovation journeys, looking at every possible movement from one quadrant to another. Based on the contextualization of this matrix, in Figure 3.2 we named each of these potential journey segments as illustrated in Figure 3.5 to help us explore the data.

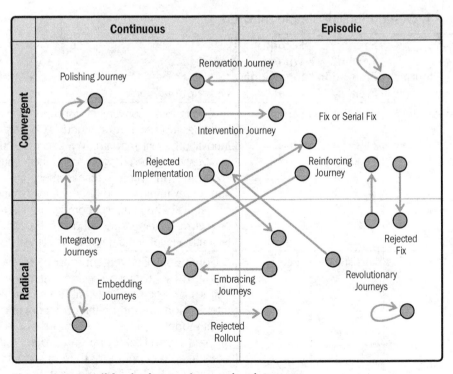

Figure 3.5. Possible single-step innovation journeys

Please note that the construction of this coding system was not as clear-cut as simply naming the simple journeys. The original coding structure had to be revised when evidence in the data suggested that the original label was not appropriate for the evidence. Therefore it was difficult to decide where to place the discussion of this operationalization. On one hand, it falls out of the operationalization of innovation events. On the other hand, the final coding structure presented here has been tested and grounded in the data. We see this coding structure as one of the contributions of this research. However, we chose to discuss it here, as it is needed as a foundation to understand the innovation journey analyses that follow.

Figure 3.5 reflects the final coding structure derived from the testing and revising of the original codes.

Possible Simple Innovation Journeys

Simple innovation journeys involve a transition from one innovation event to another. Each possible simple single-step journey illustrated in Figure 3.5 was labeled based on a two-pronged logic involving, first, a logical assessment of what the movement would entail and, second, testing this logical assertion against our data set during future analysis. Each of the labeled journeys is described in Table 3.1.

Table 3.1. Descriptions of Simple Journeys

Simple Journey Label	First Type of Innovation Event	Second Type of Innovation Event	Description
Polishing	Persistent	Persistent	A Continuous Convergent innovation event building upon a Continuous Convergent innovation event may imply a successful first intervention followed by a second intervention "polishing" the project management innovation. An example would be a first intervention of template building supporting an existing project management model and a second intervention involving training on the templates.
Fix	Persistent	Tectonic	A Continuous Convergent innovation event followed by an Episodic Convergent event implies a recognized need for an immediate intervention supporting the project management model in place. An example would be hiring a consultant to train all project managers in a short period of time in support of an ongoing PRINCE2 implementation.

Table 3.1. Descriptions of Simple Journeys *(Continued)*

Simple Journey Label	First Type of Innovation Event	Second Type of Innovation Event	Description
Rejected Implementation	Persistent	Punctuated	A Continuous Convergent innovation event followed by an Episodic Radical innovation event implies rejection of the project management model that had been implemented and a move to a completely new model, likely at the intervention of senior management. An example could be the implementation of a control oriented project management office to replace ongoing project management development efforts in support of a center of excellence project support office.
Integratory Journey	Persistent	Turbulent	Movement from a Continuous Convergent innovation event to a Continuous Radical event indicates an intervention that integrates earlier interventions to involve more people and departments in the organization. An example of such a journey could be the rolling out of a successful project management implementation at a departmental level (perhaps IT) to an organization-wide implementation.
	Turbulent	Persistent	A Continuous Radical intervention moving to a Continuous Convergent innovation event indicates the integration of what was an organization-wide project management implementation into an ongoing maintenance type innovation supporting the organization-wide implementation with more local innovations. An example of this would be an initial innovation event, such as portfolio management supported by a second innovation event improving on status reporting to support the new portfolios management.
Rejected Rollout	Turbulent	Punctuated	A Continuous Radical innovation event followed by an Episodic Radical innovation event indicates a rejection of the earlier Radical Episodic event but continuing efforts related to the ongoing innovations event. An example would be the decision to follow an organization-wide rollout of a project management model with a mandated adoption of a different project management model.

Continued

Table 3.1. Descriptions of Simple Journeys *(Continued)*

Simple Journey Label	First Type of Innovation Event	Second Type of Innovation Event	Description
Embedding Journey	Tectonic	Turbulent	An Episodic Convergent innovation event followed by a Continuous Radical innovation event indicates that the fix has been successful and the results are being rolled out to the whole organization. An example might be a training innovation event in one department that is recognized as successful and so rolled out to the whole organization.
	Turbulent	Turbulent	Continuous Radical innovation event followed by a Continuous Radical innovation event indicates a series of organization-wide project management interventions. An example would be introducing project management such as PRINCE2 to all organization projects, followed by hiring a PRINCE2-certified project manager to lead a project that would otherwise be managed by a functional manager.
Renovation	Tectonic	Persistent	Episodic Convergent innovation event to Continuous Convergent indicates that the "fix" has been accepted and the organization has moved into a period of building on and supporting the innovation. An example could be a PRINCE2 training initiative followed by a community of practice innovation event.
Rejected fix	Tectonic	Punctuated	An Episodic Convergent innovation event followed by an Episodic Radical innovation event usually indicates that the "Fix" implemented in the episodic Convergent innovation has not delivered the expected results and the decision is made to do something totally different to try to meet these needs. An example might be an effort to implement earned value project management in support of a control-oriented PMO that is followed by an initiative to implement portfolio management aimed at gaining better control of projects.

Continued

Table 3.1. Descriptions of Simple Journeys *(Continued)*

Simple Journey Label	First Type of Innovation Event	Second Type of Innovation Event	Description
Fix	Turbulent	Tectonic	A Continuous Radical innovation event followed by an Episodic Convergent innovation event suggests that the organization-wide project management innovation requires some sort of support in terms of an episodic Convergent innovation event. An example of this type of journey could be an organization-wide project management implementation event followed by investment in consultants to support the model in some way.
Serial Fix	Tectonic	Tectonic	An Episodic Convergent innovation event followed by an Episodic Convergent event usually reflects a series of "fix" activities aimed at solving the same or consecutive problems without satisfactory results. An example could be an effort to implement earned value reporting followed by an initiative aimed at reporting project reporting.
Revolutionary	Punctuated	Persistent	An Episodic Radical innovation followed by Continuous Convergent innovations implies an organization-wide effort to improve the new project management model. An example is a regulated adoption of a project management model followed by polishing and shaping activity aimed at making the model fit the needs of the organization.
Embracing	Punctuated	Turbulent	An Episodic Radical event followed by a Continuous Radical event suggests the infrastructure is being built in support of an organization-wide change in project management models. An example would be the decision to adopt a new project management model such as PRINCE2 or the *PMBOK® Guide*, followed by establishment of a corporate PMO to support these changes.

Continued

Table 3.1. Descriptions of Simple Journeys *(Continued)*

Simple Journey Label	First Type of Innovation Event	Second Type of Innovation Event	Description
Reinforcing Journey	Punctuated	Tectonic	An Episodic Radical innovation followed by an Episodic Convergent innovation suggests the first organization-wide innovation event needs support from an innovation event that is Convergent with existing project management models.
Volatile journey	Punctuated	Punctuated	An Episodic Radical event followed by an Episodic Radical event suggests a lot of uncertainty at the top levels of the organization with respect to the direction for project management in an organization. An example might be where a CIO decides to roll out *PMBOK® Guide*-flavored project management and a new CIO comes in and changes the direction to a PRINCE2 implementation.

Complex Innovation Journeys

Complex innovation journeys involve multiple innovation events within one organization over a period of time. The linked series of innovation events provides the opportunity to examine the dynamics and evolution of implementation journeys over time, as well as the triggers and sociopolitical and behavioral elements of innovation.

Chapter Summary

As stated in the last chapter, innovation is a difficult phenomenon to study, for many reasons. In this chapter we are interested in the difficulty of operationalizing "management innovation," rather than the difficulty in theorizing the phenomenon. Drawing from organizational change and innovation literature, we describe the operationalizations that allow us to examine management innovation as a specific form of organizational change, made up of innovation events that are intentionally enacted in an effort to implement new ways of thinking about, practicing, or regulating project management within the target organization. Drawing on this important literature, we pay particular attention to the events involved in the innovation journey and the people, triggers, and contexts that influence the accepted or challenged outcomes of these events. The coding structure for labeling innovation journey structures is both a contribution to the literature and an empirical finding of this study.

The next chapter provides details on the empirical basis for this study, including the nature of the data available to us, the coding and preparation of the data, and the analytic techniques used to make sense of the data.

Chapter 4

Empirical Evidence and Methods

Some suggest that a longitudinal study over many years is the ideal approach to such an initiative, allowing researchers to collect data through the entire process of initiation, adoption, and implementation within one organization (Van de Ven & Poole, 2005). However, longitudinal studies of this type are notoriously difficult to manage, as well as time- and resource-intensive. An alternative approach, more practical but executed with similar infrequency, was suggested by Birkinshaw and Mol (2006): it involves studying the same innovation in multiple case studies, thereby examining organizations at different stages in the same innovation journey.

We adopted the second approach, using a quasi-experimental design (Grant & Wall, 2009), based on multiple comparative case studies (Eisenhardt, 1989; Eisenhardt & Graebner, 2007), in order to retroactively explore histories of project management implementations constructed using multiple sources of information. Each case history explored all of the innovation events, and contained links that joined innovation events to journeys and organizational performance.

Following Eisenhardt's philosophy that "it is the connection with empirical reality that permits the development of a testable, relevant, and valid theory" (1989, p. 29), and attempting to honor Van Maanen's desire for case research to be "empirical enough to be credible and analytical enough to be interesting" (1988, p. 29), we set out to encapsulate, compare, and contrast the experience of many organizations engaged in implementing a common management innovation—specifically, the improvement of the management of project work.

This chapter provides an introduction to the data, methods, and sample used in this study. While we drew from the extant literature relating to organizational change and innovation as described in Chapter 2, the methods we used in examining each individual innovation event and journey were unique to this study. In extending the Street and Gallupe model (2009) to examine not just the pace and scope of the entirety of a change journey, but also the events and their linkages over the course of each innovation journey—and to do so for multiple organizations—led us to realize that we needed to explore new ways to prepare and look at an extensive, largely qualitative, data set. Our use of a case-study database, data preparation, and sample selection were also quite complex, and required a substantial amount of analysis. As the following discussion will demonstrate, our method is thus in itself one of the study's significant contributions to the field.

Data

The data used in this research is drawn from a case-study database that includes 65 organizations. It was collected between 2006 and 2008 using a multi-method approach (on-site observations, interviews, surveys, and archival document review). Although not explicitly collected to study innovation journeys, this data was rich in information about the process of innovation that had been used by these organizations in project management. Three cases were updated through interviews to examine the innovation events or outcomes that had occurred in the intervening period (2009 to 2011) between the original data capture and this research.

In order to examine the process of innovation implementation in as much detail as possible, we use two types of data from this data set. The first described the dynamics of the innovation journey itself through the reported evidence of the organizational participants. Details of how this reported data was collected using the mixed-method research design, and an inventory of the types of data and size of the database, can be found in Thomas and Mullaly (2008).

The second type of data was required to support the assertion that management innovation involves an investment in practice change designed to deliver beneficial outcomes. In prior analysis (Thomas & Mullaly, 2008), each of these cases was coded by multiple researchers according to four measures of what are arguably the value outcomes of any project management implementation:

- Maturity level, coded on the basis of a generic five-stage maturity model that allowed for half-step increments
- Value trend, ranging from −2 ("most recent interventions are actively and substantially decreasing value of project management to the organization") to +2 ("clear evidence that most recent interventions are expected to deliver value long into the future"), coded on the basis of the likelihood of the organization's continuing to receive value from its last project management intervention
- Intangible benefits, coded on a scale of −2 (no evidence) to +2 (evidence of significant benefits), based on available information that the organization had received intangible benefits (improved management decision-making, improved culture, improved reputation, or greater legitimacy, to name a few)
- Tangible benefits, coded on a scale of −2 (no evidence) to +2 (evidence of significant benefits), based on information showing that measurable, tangible benefits had been received that could be attributed to the last project management intervention

This second type of data in particular allowed exploration of outcomes, as it evaluated the benefits reported by the case organizations as a result of their implementation of an innovation.

Methods

The analysis of this data involved four separate steps, described in the following sections.

Step 1: Data Preparation and Construction of Journey Maps

The innovation journey of an organization—as conceptualized in Chapter 3—tells a tale of not only what and how innovations were put in place, but also indicates why the specific innovation action was chosen. In order to construct journey maps, we first identified events from the multiple case-data sources and then arranged them into a time line. Using the information from this identification-and-time analysis, these events were linked into a sequence; thereby, the journey of innovation for each case organization was represented graphically.

The details of this analytical process are provided in the steps outlined below.

Selection of Appropriate Cases—From 65 to 48

Each of the 65 studies was examined in detail to identify cases with enough information to answer the types of questions we were raising in this study. We identified a subset of 48 cases for further examination on the basis that they contained rich detail about the triggers, timelines, key individuals, and events involved in each of the respective organization's project management implementation.

Identification of Events

Next, data sources (interview notes, research-case write-ups, survey responses, archival documents, etc.) for each of the 48 cases were examined to identify distinct events involved in a project management innovation. As explained in Chapter 3, an "innovation event" is described in terms of the trigger, goal, actions, and outcomes that are associated with it. The environment of an organization creates continual triggers for change. Time passes while a trigger becomes important enough to be detected, goals are set, action is taken, and outcomes are experienced.

For this research, each innovation event was identified by two researchers, who described the event in terms of its trigger, the goals for the innovation intervention, the actual innovation activity, and the outcomes of that activity. They then characterized the event in terms of pace and scope. An example of this coding structure for one event is provided in Table 4.1.

This analysis resulted in a database of over 100 events across the 48 organizations, spanning a 30-year time frame.

Table 4.1. Example of a Coded Intervention for One Case Organization

	1988
Trigger	Extreme complexity and risks of mega-projects as well as high market-competition pressure. The predominant culture in the organization is customer- and investor-focused.
Goals	To realize the goals of projects and improve project implementation efficiency.
What	Implementation of project management in mega-infrastructure projects: developing pre-period project management software, investing RMB5, 714/person in project management training each year.
Outcomes	High customer satisfaction to the project results (4.33/5), maintain long-term customer relationship, improve brand image (low level of environmental destruction and disturbance), and abilities of employees can get a good and rapid development through project management implementation. Through project management project goals were successfully realized, and costs were decreased.
Pace	Episodic
Scope	Radical

Construction of Timelines

Using an Excel spreadsheet, we created an Innovation Events Timeline. Each organization's innovation events were then situated on the timeline, indicating the sequence in which they occurred. Each organization's innovation journey was documented in one line of this spreadsheet.

Methodologically, deciding when to call something a "journey" is problematic. In the current study, we included every innovation event that involved an investment to improve project management practice in the organization's journey. Reviewing the history of interventions for an organization, it is not always clear whether one or several journeys have occurred. Two cases in particular in this study seemed to have more than one journey within their overall innovation. The case narratives of Chapter 6 and the case discussion in Chapter 7 consider this situation more deeply. The Innovation Events Timeline Excel spreadsheet was large and cumbersome to analyze, but it did allow us to pull different views of the cases, which in turn allowed us to conduct cross-case comparisons easily on variables of interest. We were able, for example, to compare activities in historical or relative time, and to conduct detailed analyses of cases exhibiting different paces or scopes of change over time. (Note: Due to confidentiality and size considerations, this spreadsheet is not included in this monograph.)

Construction of Pictorial Representations

The full timeline of each case was then converted to a pictorial representation of the innovation journey for the case organization. This was done by positioning each innovation event, with respect to its pace and scope categorization, on Figure 3.2, derived by Street and Gallupe (2009) from Plowman et al. (2007), as described in Chapter 3 (see Figure 3.1), to illustrate the operationalization of change in terms of

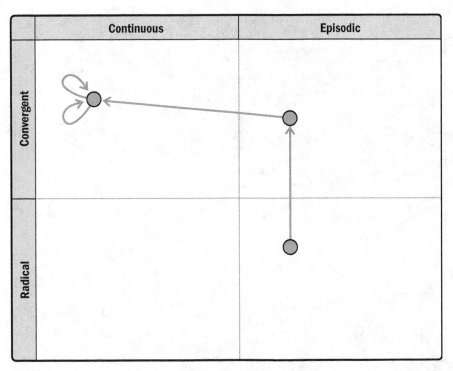

Figure 4.1. An example (Case 23) of a map showing a compound innovation journey.

pace and scope. Each innovation event was then linked in temporal order to show the sequence of innovation events within its overall innovation journey. The journey map created represents the sequence of innovation events for each case organization graphically (see example, Figure 4.1). Each innovation event is located on the map with a circle, and the transition between events is depicted by a line that joins them; the line's arrow indicates the direction of each segment in the innovation journey. In cases where there is an event-to-event transition of the same pace and scope, the events are superimposed to show each of the journeys occurring in a cluster.

Some organizations' innovation journeys were simple; others were multi-stage and complex. Although each innovation journey is unique to an organization, distinct classes of innovation journey were identified in this visualization. Journey segments were also identified and labeled, as discussed in Chapter 3.

Figure 4.2 represents our first attempt to visualize together, on one diagram, the 48 innovation journey maps that make up our data set. This photograph suggests the complexity and magnitude of the data that formed the foundation for our study. Mapping all 48 cases on one diagram allowed us to begin to see the patterns, similarities and differences among the journeys. From this starting point, we were able to identify important areas for further analysis using the concepts described in Chapter 3 and to begin to group cases for further study.

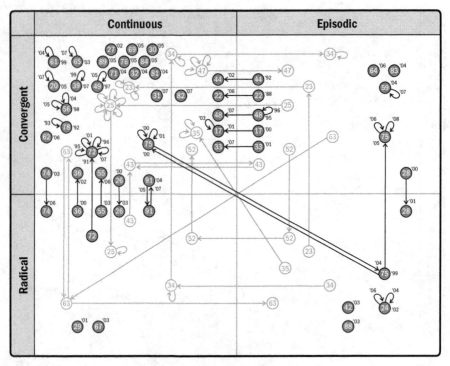

Figure 4.2. Mapping of innovation journeys of the 48 cases in the study.

Step 2: Descriptive Analysis of 48 Cases

Based on the timelines and pictorial representations of the 48 cases, we conducted a descriptive analysis of each of the innovation journeys. The historical timelines allowed us to compare innovation journeys for "relatively recent" versus "later" adopters, and to examine the nature of the journeys over time in terms of the types and number of events undertaken. We examined the nature of each project management innovation event undertaken, and by normalizing the time scale of each organization's sequence of innovations, we were able to investigate variations in the phases of project management implementation across the data set. The results of this analysis are presented in Chapter 5.

Step 3: Selection of Ten Cases For Further Study

During the review of the timelines of the 48 cases, we began to identify classes of innovation journey (from the journey-map visualization), themes associated with different value outcomes, and the value trends associated with each journey.

Innovation journeys with more interventions provided data around the activity of innovating, and information around the dynamics of the innovation journey, that is applicable to the process of sense-making and furthering our understanding of project management as a management innovation. After analyzing the 48 cases as described above, we identified a subset of 10 detailed implementation journeys supported by additional data on which to focus further analysis. Each of these 10 cases selected for detailed consideration had experienced complex journeys involving four or more reported innovation events (Cases 23, 25, 35, 43, 47, 52, 72, and 75), or was a case for which the researchers had extensive data and associated knowledge (Cases 34 and 63) that could be extended and updated by interviews to reflect the events that had occurred after the initial data capture had been completed in 2008. In addition, each of the 10 cases exhibited interesting value or maturity outcomes that made them particularly good candidates for furthering our understanding of the project management innovation journey.

Descriptive statistics for each of these 10 case studies is provided in Table 4.2.

Step 4: Construction of Case Narratives

Each researcher examined the pictorial representation of each case organization's innovation journey and compared this picture to the documentation for the case and the list of themes derived from the literature review included in Chapter 2. Each innovation event depicted in the journey map was described in Table 4.3 by date, innovation made, event type (based on the Event Matrix from Figure 3.2), plus the journey segment type (characterized in Figure 3.4).

Case narratives were then drafted for each journey by each researcher and compared for common and consistent understanding. The detailed discussion of each of the 10 journeys, along with iterative returns to the data sources, resulted in additional new narratives of each journey being created, weaving together joint and separate sense-making of the interviews, case descriptions, and archival data. They included a methodological check of comparisons of researchers' observations with our growing lists of themes, following the advice of Miles and Huberman (1994). In total, each journey was analyzed and the narrative enriched up to six times by a total of four different researchers over a period of 12 months. The iterative development of these narratives through triangulation between data sources and researcher perspectives served to strengthen the reliability of the interpretations.

Through triangulation, narrative analysis, pictorial representation and discussion, we were able to observe patterns within the data relating to the types of innovation events, and the patterning of these events across time. This comparative case approach (Eisenhardt & Graebner, 2007) allowed us to develop theoretical insights into the patterns of relationships among constructs (innovation events, journey segments, innovation journeys) defined in Chapter 3 and those emerging from the situated action within and across cases related to underlying logics of actions. Building theory from cases requires looking at each case as a distinct experiment that serves as a replication; researchers can then contrast and compare constraints and develop extensions to the emerging theory (Yin, 2003).

Detailed case narratives for each of the 10 innovation journeys are presented in Chapter 6.

Table 4.2. Selected Case Descriptions

	Country	Culture	Competition	Industry	Project Type	Value trend	Tangible Value	Intangible Value	Researchers' Views on Project Management in Case Organization
23	China	Entrepreneurial, customer- and investor-focused	Very high	IT	Customer	Positive (1)	Some (2)	Some (2)	This is a project-based organization; almost every person in the company was involved in the project management improvement.
25	Denmark	Innovative and competitive	Medium	IT	Customer	Strong positive (2)	Some (2)	Some (2)	Project management provides a common frame of reference for knowledge-sharing, allowing high quality, customer satisfaction.
34	UK			Education					Formal project management is seen as valuable only to some in this organization.
35	China	Customer- and investor-focused	High	Construction	Customer	Strong positive (2)	Most (3)	Most (3)	Project management capability matches customer, subcontractor and supplier expectations.
43	Australia	Innovative, customer- and stakeholder-focused	Medium	Government	Product/customer/internal	Neutral (0)	None (0)	Some (2)	Project management is central to the organization's existence; if it doesn't deliver successful projects, it will no longer exist.

	Country	Culture	Competition	Industry	Project Type	Value trend	Tangible Value	Intangible Value	Researchers' Views on Project Management in Case Organization
47	UK	Customer- and stakeholder-focused	N/A	Defense, aerospace	Customer, product	Negative (−1)	Most (3)	Few (1)	This organization is happy with what it has in place. There does not, however, appear to be a fit between what the parent organization and the case-study organization management tell us about the practice of project management, and the actual observed practice and attitudes toward project management.
52	Denmark	Strongly professional with some silos of knowledge	Medium	Pharmaceutical	Product, customer	Neutral (0)	None (0)	Some (2)	
63	Canada	Growth and entrepreneurship	Medium/high	Energy	Internal	Positive (1)	None (0)	Most (3)	Fits strategy, formal but grounded
72	China	N/A	High	Construction/energy	Internal	Positive (1)	Some (2)	Most (3)	
75	Canada	N/A	Medium	Energy		Negative (−2)	Some (2)	Some (1)	

Further background information on these 10 cases is included in the Appendix.

Table 4.3. An Example (Case 23) of Detailed Timing and Type Analysis of Innovation Events

Date	Date	Event Type (Pace and Scope)	Journey Segment Type
1999	ISO9001 to achieve formal planning and control	Punctuated (Episodic and Radical)	Reinforcing
2004	CMM3—a more formalized project management function and assurance of quality	Tectonic (Episodic and Convergent)	Renovating
2005	Status reporting and scoring system	Persistent (Continuous and Convergent)	Polishing
2007	Lesson learned database	Persistent (Continuous and Convergent)	Polishing
2008	Training program	Persistent (Continuous and Convergent)	

Chapter Summary

Methodologically, management innovation is recognized as a difficult process to examine. In this chapter we have outlined the frameworks we developed—based on the literature reviewed in Chapter 2—for the conceptualization of innovation events characterized by pace and scope, and the links among innovation events and innovation journeys. In this chapter we have also presented the data with which we worked, and outlined the preliminary methods we used to prepare the data for analysis. We have explained the methods of analysis used in developing findings that were grounded in the data.

As noted in Chapter 2, our operationalization of the process of management innovation, as exemplified by project management implementations, captures many elements recognized in innovation theory and contributes additional approaches to research design for management innovation studies. The methods detailed in this chapter show how innovation journeys can be examined, and more specifically how the linkages among context, events, triggers, dynamics, and journey segments can be explicitly examined, both visually and through descriptive statistics.

We turn now, in Chapter 5, to the detailed examination of the results of Step 2— that is, the descriptive analyses of the 48 innovation journeys. Chapter 6 presents the results of steps 3 and 4, the narratives of the 10 compound innovation journeys.

Chapter 5

Exploring 48 Innovation Journeys

In this chapter we consider the 48 innovation journeys that were available to us for analysis. Starting with an overview of descriptive statistics for these journeys, we begin by describing the event sample. Starting with an overview of descriptive statistics for these journeys, we embrace the idea (from Chapter 3) by describing the innovation journeys as combinations of innovation events. We begin by looking at the beginning and ending events in each journey. We continue by describing the simple and complex innovation journeys. Throughout this chapter we highlight the kinds of questions this level of analysis raised for us that required deeper analysis. Finally we identify the 10 compound cases we selected for further study.

Descriptive Statistics

Of the 48 case organizations, four began their investment in project management in the 1980s, 11 in the 1990s, and 33 in the 2000s (see Table 5.1). With only nine early adopters (those organizations investing in project management for 20 or more years), this may seem like a skewed sample, but when you consider the exponential growth in membership in organizations such as the Project Management Institute (from fewer than 8,000 members in the 1980s to over 350,000 today), the rapid growth in the workplace of technology and use of information technology, and the impact that the millennium had on project demands, this sampling seems to reasonably reflect the growth in adoption and use of project management over this period.

Table 5.1. Number of Organizations' Initial Project Management Journeys, by Decade

	<1990s	1990s	2000s
Number	4	11	33

Similarly in Table 5.2, the number of cases by decade reflects that innovation in project management was recent or ongoing for many organizations with an "end" seen in relatively few case organizations.

Table 5-2. Number of Organizations' Latest Interventions in Project Management Journey, By Decade

	1990s	<2005	>=2005
Number of Cases	3	15	31

As Table 5.3 shows, of the 48 innovation journeys, the majority of cases had simple journeys (fewer than three innovation events).

Table 5-3. Number of Journeys by Number of Innovation Events

Events in Journey	Number of Cases
1	18
2	15
3	5
4	2
5	4
6	1
7	1
8	0
9	1
10	1

Preliminary Journey Analysis

Many cases started and/or ended with Persistent events (Continuous and Convergent activities), reflecting improvements to existing project management models and approaches.

Journey Beginnings

Earlier research (Thomas et al., 2002) provided evidence that in the period leading up to 2000, senior-management interest in project management was highest when the intervention was driven by external events. These external events led to significant Episodic, and likely Radical, innovations. Looking at the initial intervention in

Table 5.4. Pace and Scope of First and Latest Innovation Events

Scope	Pace	
	Continuous	**Episodic**
Convergent	PERSISTENT	TECTONIC
	Started Persistent: 22 (45.8%)	Started Tectonic: 12 (25%)
	Ended Persistent: 31 (64.6%)	Ended Tectonic: 6 (12.5%)
	Solely Persistent: 19 (39.6%)	Solely Tectonic: 3 (6.2%)
Radical	TURBULENT	PUNCTUATED
	Started Turbulent: 7 (14.6%)	Started Punctuated: 7 (14.6%)
	Ended Turbulent: 6 (12.5%)	Ended Punctuated: 5 (10.4%)
	Solely Turbulent: 2 (4.2%)	Solely Punctuated: 3 (6.2%)

our 48 organizations (see Table 5.4), we see that 39.6% of our cases did in fact begin in this way. However, over 44.8% of these innovation journeys, a much higher proportion than expected, began with Continuous Convergent interventions focused on improving existing practices and frameworks over time, rather than in more dramatic or externally imposed interventions. Of the 39.6%, 25% of the interventions began as Episodic/Convergent efforts aimed at solving a problem with the existing project management practices, using improvements that were consistent with the existing project management models; 14.6% were associated with more Radical interventions aimed at fundamentally changing the project management models in use in all areas of the organization. The remaining 14.6% of the first project management interventions were associated with undertakings tied to moving project management into an organization-wide activity.

These results do provide support for the 2002 study by Thomas et al. which found that nearly 40% of organizations did innovate in response to internal events, but 45% did not, and that raises questions about what might be driving the Continuous improvement of existing models to be the most common project management innovation journey. The focus on Continuous improvement of existing models seems to indicate that these organizations were ignoring the advice offered by an increasing body of practitioner and academic literature (Morris & Jamieson, 2005; Shenhar & Dvir, 2007; Srivannaboon & Milosevic, 2006), which has asserted the need for project management to move beyond improving project management alone to reach a more strategic level, and to effect new functions and levels of the organization—such as program, portfolio, and enterprise initiatives—which will require interventions that are considered more Radical in nature. This finding supports the innovation theory discussed in Chapter 2 in demonstrating that the reality of project management implementation today does not follow the advice of existing literature. This does not imply necessarily that the advice is wrong: it could be that current management innovation around project management practice is not meeting the needs identified by researchers.

Latest Recorded Intervention

Perhaps not surprisingly, the latest recorded interventions for each case (see Table 5.4) were even more biased toward Persistent (Convergent/Continuous) interventions than the initial interventions. As an innovation journey learns its way to improved practice, one could expect that later innovation events would be aimed at building on and expanding the practices devised through earlier innovation events.

We might have been more surprised by the number of instances where the final intervention recorded in our cases was Episodic, that is, where the interventions were seen to disrupt the existing practice. However, the literature review in Chapter 2 reminds us that the final stages of the innovation cycle—where organizations attempt adaptation, routinization, stabilization, and sustainability—are often the most unpredictable and dynamic. Therefore we can expect to see Episodic events erupting from Continuous Convergent routinization activities.

In total, 77.1% (64.6% Persistent plus 12.5% Tectonic) of the latest project management innovations, in this set of organizations, converged with the existing models and understanding of project management that had previously existed in the organization when the innovation was undertaken. This seems to indicate that the level of novelty in these innovation interventions was relatively low. It also suggests that a convergence of practice may be occurring as a result of mimetic behavior and the work of professional and educational associations in encouraging the standardization of practice.

Examining the latest innovation events more carefully, we found that in 18 cases they were also the first innovation for the case organization (see Table 5.3) In these 18 single-event innovations, there were 2 examples for each of Tectonic, Turbulent, and Episodic innovation types, and 12 cases were a Persistent innovation (see Table 5.6). All of these case's first innovations were put in place in the 2000s. This overlapping set of first and latest innovations did not indicate that an organization would only ever have a single-step journey—we may just have sampled at the beginning of an organization's journey.

Additionally the fact that so many of these latest innovating organizations started at the same point that other organizations ended—with Persistent events—suggests that more organizations in the 2000s than in 80s and 90s are both beginning and ending their project management innovation journeys by investing in interventions aimed at incrementally improving the existing practices and frameworks of project management. The implications of this finding will be explored in greater detail in the exploration of innovation journeys in Chapter 7 and in our discussions in Chapter 8.

Taking a wider view, 41.7% of all innovation journeys in our study both had Persistent events that built on existing project management activities as their first and latest innovations. (It should be noted that not all first innovations remain in Persistent and not all latest innovation events began there.) It is also worth noting that 81% of journeys have at least one Persistent intervention. Clearly, Continuous Convergent types of innovation events, whereby management innovation activity supports or enhances existing practices, rather than disrupting existing organizational activity, are an important component of project management implementations. Bringing in external project management practices, and the adoption of external best practices, may be one way to account for this propensity to continuously converge, especially in the 2000s, where there is a clearer standardized idea of what best practice should be. When an organization assumes it is starting from the best position possible, all that remains is to tweak the implementation to fit the organization slightly better. At the same time, we also note that more than 50% (28 in total) of all 48 innovation journeys in the sample had first and latest innovation events of the same type. This may suggest a tendency for organizations to repeat history or prefer a specific type of intervention that fits more closely with their culture or context. Future research could pursue this line of thought.

Simple Project Management Implementation Journeys

Eighteen organizations (see Table 5.5) had only invested in one managerial innovation aimed at improving project management practice at the time of the research study. Each of these 18 had begun investing in project management in 2001 or later, and so could be identified as recent adopters. Examining the nature of these interventions provided insight into the level of novelty associated with project management innovations in the last decade.

All the organizations that reported only one innovation event appeared to be at a relatively low level of project management maturity (scoring 1 to 2 out of 5 on a maturity rating, Thomas & Mullaly, 2008), and reported significant intangible benefits from their investment. Most of those conducting customer-oriented projects also reported some tangible benefits, and reported additionally that they expected a continued positive value trend from their investment. This result reflects the literature in Chapter 2 that pointed out the importance of recognizing innovation events as conscious activities aimed at gaining positive improvements to practice. However six organizations report an "undetermined" value trend and one organization reported negative value from its investment. The turbulence and uncertainty associated with positive outcomes again reflects the difficulty of successfully implementing management innovation, as discussed in Chapter 2.

Fully 67% of the relatively recent innovation events (occurring within three years of data collection) were characterized as Persistent events of a Continuous

Table 5.5. Single-Innovation Cases

Case Number	Case Location	Industry	Project Type	Start/ End Year	Start/ End Type
27	Germany	Financial IT Services	Product	2002	Persistent
29	Canada	Government	Customer/internal	2001	Turbulent
30	Canada	Energy	Product	2005	Persistent
31	Serbia	Consultancy	Customer	2007	Persistent
32	Lithuania	Security Services	Customer/internal	2004	Persistent
42	Australia	Government	Product/customer/internal	2003	Punctuated
62	USA	Manufacturing	Product	2006	Persistent
64	Brazil	Government	Internal	2006	Tectonic
67	UAE	Construction	Customer	2003	Turbulent
69	UAE	Construction Engineering	Customer	2005	Persistent
71	USA	Construction	Customer	2004	Persistent
76	Canada	Consulting	Customer	2005	Persistent
81	Brazil	Consulting	Customer	2004	Persistent
82	Brazil	Engineering	Customer	2007	Persistent
83	UK	Pharmaceutical	Product	2004	Tectonic
84	Brazil	Energy	Customer	2005	Persistent
88	Russia	Food	Internal	2003	Punctuated
89	Russia	IT	Customer	2005	Persistent

Convergent nature, suggesting, as discussed above, that these most recent innovators were drawing from industry-specified or "best practice" interventions that supported their existing project management practice in an effort to improve it. However, this data does not indicate whether these innovation events were the final (as well as first) for these organizations, as the events could reflect the beginnings of more substantial journeys. Careful review of the data suggests that this may well be the case for

Table 5.6. Single Innovation Event Journeys by Event Type

Scope	Pace	
	Continuous	**Episodic**
Convergent	PERSISTENT	TECTONIC
	12 Cases (67%)	2 cases (11%)
Radical	TURBULENT	PUNCTUATED
	2 cases (11%)	2 cases (11%)

many of the case organizations, in that the respective study participants mentioned future innovations they expected to make.

One innovation journey occurred as early as 2001 and consisted of a single Turbulent intervention. The organization reported significant intangible and ongoing benefits from its introduction of project management, and reported no need for

Table 5.7. Cases Beginning Innovation Journey After 2001

Case Number	Case Location	Start Year	Start Type	End Year	End Type	Number of Events
29	Canada	2001	Turbulent	2001	Turbulent	1
33	Serbia	2001	Tectonic	2007	Persistent	2
91	Serbia	2001	Turbulent	2005	Turbulent	3
24	China	2002	Punctuated	2006	Punctuated	3
27	Germany	2002	Persistent	2002	Persistent	1
42	Australia	2003	Punctuated	2003	Punctuated	1
55	USA	2003	Turbulent	2006	Persistent	2
65	Brazil	2003	Persistent	2007	Persistent	2
67	UAE	2003	Turbulent	2003	Turbulent	1
74	China	2003	Persistent	2006	Turbulent	2
88	Russia	2003	Punctuated	2003	Punctuated	1
32	Lithuania	2004	Persistent	2004	Persistent	1
59	Canada	2004	Tectonic	2007	Tectonic	2
71	USA	2004	Persistent	2004	Persistent	1
81	Brazil	2004	Persistent	2004	Persistent	1
83	UK	2004	Tectonic	2004	Tectonic	1
20	Canada	2005	Persistent	2007	Persistent	2
30	Canada	2005	Persistent	2005	Persistent	1
69	UAE	2005	Persistent	2005	Persistent	1
76	Canada	2005	Persistent	2005	Persistent	1
84	Brazil	2005	Persistent	2005	Persistent	1
89	Russia	2005	Persistent	2005	Persistent	1
34	UK	2006	Punctuated	2008	Tectonic	7
62	USA	2006	Persistent	2006	Persistent	1
64	Brazil	2006	Tectonic	2006	Tectonic	1
31	Serbia	2007	Persistent	2007	Persistent	1
63	Canada	2007	Tectonic	2010	Punctuated	5
82	Brazil	2007	Persistent	2007	Persistent	1

further innovation. This case seemed to run counter to innovation theory discussed in Chapter 2, where it was suggested that sustaining management innovation requires constant effort. However, further exploration of the case indicated that the project management practice has been routinized into the learning organization culture, such that improvements to project management are seen as a normal part of their practice, and are not identified as an additional intervention.

Recent Innovation Events

Twenty-eight of our 48 cases had adopted project management as a management innovation since 2001. Of these, the journeys of only two included more than four innovation events (these cases will be studied in more detail) compared to the 18 in the previous section that had only one innovation event.

We might expect these relatively recent adopters to have been more influenced by their institutional context than were the early adopters, and to follow a common recipe or standards-based approach to implementing project management. We might also expect that their first implementations might involve "proof of concept" or an effort to gain benefit from "low-hanging fruit" types of interventions. It was also deemed highly likely that these late adopters would follow the experience of earlier adopters or external consultants. Indeed, the majority of these organizations opted for a Persistent type (blue) innovation that focused on the management of projects and the adaptation of current processes in an incremental manner—often by adopting some project management standard to gain legitimacy for their project management innovation. The kinds of innovations these organizations invested in are illustrated in Table 5.8.

Table 5.8. Innovations Undertaken By Recent (Since 2001) Adopters

Scope	Pace	
	Continuous-Adaptive	**Episodic-Focused on Increasing**
Convergent-focused on project management	PERSISTENT	TECTONIC
	23 events, 20 cases (71.4%)	8 events, 6 cases (21.4%)
	1 (2002, 2008); 2 (2003); 3 (2006); 4 (2004); 6 (2005, 2007)	1 (2001, 2006); 2 (2004, 2007, 2008)
	Focused on improving projects	Focused on improving throughput
Radical-focused on organizational management	TURBULENT	PUNCTUATED
	9 events, 7 cases (25%)	7 events, 5 cases (17.9%)
	1 (2001, 2002, 2005, 2009); 2 (2003); 3 (2006)	1 (2002, 2003, 2010); 2 (2004, 2006)
	Focused on managing by projects	Imposed to meet external drivers

Early Innovators

Of the 20 organizations that adopted project management as a management innovation in 2000 or earlier (see Table 5.9), seven (Cases 22, 25, 39, 43, 44, 72, and 73) had been investing in project management for 20 years or more (it is possible that others in this group had simply not reported their earliest project management innovations). As noted in the literature, defining the boundaries of an innovation journey is not a straightforward activity and some organizations may have longer memories, or may tie past journeys into the new journeys, while others may latch on to a specific event as the start of a journey.

Table 5.9. Cases Adopting Project Management Innovations Before Year 2000

Case Number	Case Location	Start Year	Start Type	End Year	End Type	Number of Events
17	Denmark	2000	Tectonic	2003	Persistent	3
22	China	1988	Tectonic	2006	Persistent	2
23	China	1999	Punctuated	2008	Persistent	5
25	Denmark	1985	Tectonic	2007	Turbulent	11
26	Denmark	2000	Persistent	2007	Turbulent	2
28	Serbia	2000	Tectonic	2001	Punctuated	2
35	China	1995	Punctuated	2006	Persistent	5
6	China	2000	Turbulent	2002	Persistent	2
39	China	1957	Persistent	1999	Persistent	2
43	Australia	1990	Turbulent	2007	Persistent	4
44	Australia	1992	Tectonic	2002	Persistent	2
47	UK	1996	Persistent	2003	Tectonic	5
48	Denmark	1995	Tectonic	2007	Persistent	3
49	Canada	1997	Persistent	2005	Persistent	2
52	Denmark	2000	Tectonic	2007	Persistent	4
56	China	1998	Persistent	2005	Persistent	3
61	USA	1999	Persistent	2004	Persistent	2
72	China	1988	Turbulent	2007	Persistent	5
73	China	1992	Persistent	1993	Persistent	2
75	Canada	1999	Punctuated	2008	Tectonic	9

Of these 20 cases, eight had complex journeys comprising four or more innovations. Given our interest in the implementation of innovation and the dynamics of this process, we decided that of all the cases studied, these complex journeys were most likely to provide us with detailed information about who did what, when and why. Therefore, these eight cases were selected for further study.

In addition, one of these cases (Case 75) and two other cases (34 and 63) were updated to 2011 using interviews, in order to provide a sample of 10 complex innovation journeys for further exploration. The depth of data collected around these 10 cases can be used to further the sense-making around the dynamics of the innovation process. Table 5.10 provides a summary of the cases that were chosen for further analysis. These analyses are discussed in Chapter 6.

Table 5.10. Case Journey for Cases With Four or More Innovation Events

Case Number	Case Location	Start Year	Start Type	End Year	End Type	Number of Events
23	China	1999	Punctuated	2008	Persistent	5
25	Denmark	1985	Tectonic	2007	Turbulent	11
34	UK	2006	Punctuated	2008	Tectonic	7
35	China	1995	Punctuated	2006	Persistent	5
43	Australia	1990	Turbulent	2007	Persistent	4
47	UK	1996	Persistent	2003	Tectonic	5
52	Denmark	2000	Tectonic	2007	Persistent	4
63	Canada	2007	Tectonic	2010	Punctuated	5
72	China	1988	Turbulent	2007	Persistent	5
75	Canada	1999	Punctuated	2008	Tectonic	9

Chapter Summary

In this chapter we described the 48 cases that formed the first stage of our research study. Our cases spanned a 30-year period, in 12 countries, and were representative of the types of organizations implementing project management over this period. Those organizations in the study that had been investing in project management for the longest time had typically begun their journeys in order to address strong external demands (regulation, funding, customers), and they reported more Radical and Episodic innovations than more recent innovators. The more recent innovators focused on innovation events that were consistent and Convergent directed at integrating external standards or models of project management into existing practices. This likely reflected maturing institutional influences on project management (including professional associations, consultants, trainers, education programs) that are evident today. Of the earlier interventions in a journey, many were in response to external events requiring significant Episodic and/or Radical innovations. Later interventions, as with later innovators, focused on Continuous Convergent (Persistent) innovation events.

Single-innovation journeys that happened close to our data collection period are ambiguous as to whether they are complete journeys in and of themselves or whether they are the start of a more complex journey. The majority (67%) was characterized as Continuous events of a Continuous Convergent nature. We believe this is a conscious activity to generate improvement in practice while minimizing turbulence and uncertainty. In most cases, these organizations are relying on industry of professional identification of "best practices" or standards to serve as the foundation and trigger for innovation. There are inherent issues with this approach that are discussed in Chapter 8.

We went on to perform preliminary analysis of the 48 cases in terms of where their journeys of innovation began and where they took the organizations involved. We noted that the latest reported innovation was not necessarily the end of the journey for these organizations. We also noted that some innovations were more complex than others. These will be considered in further detail in Chapter 6.

This preliminary analysis raised some interesting methodological concerns for the study of innovation. We noted that it was difficult to identify the first innovation, given the lack of organizational memory in some organizations. This makes innovation journeys difficult to compare across organizations. In addition, classifying the nature of an innovation is complicated by the theoretical recognition, discussed in Chapter 2, that an innovation does not need to be new to the world but may be new solely to the people involved in the event. As a result, what for one group would not be considered innovation—or at best might be seen only as an improvement to current practice (Continuous Convergent)—for another could easily be seen as Episodic or even Radical. Finding a way to explore the complexities of these journeys across a large number of organizations is challenging. To further our understanding of the dynamics of the innovation process and address some of these challenges requires a more detailed assessment of the data.

We now turn to Chapter 6, in which we present a detailed examination of 10 complex case journeys. These cases were selected based on steps 3 and 4 outlined in Chapter 4 and the preliminary analysis undertaken here in Chapter 5. The detail of these cases allowed us to undertake a sense-making exercise around the interweaving factors that influence innovation and the dynamics of the process.

Chapter 6

Ten Complex Innovation Journeys

As noted in Chapters 2 and 3, innovation is a difficult phenomenon to study, because it is embedded in a complex web of organizational activity, and tends to be unique to the situation under study. This chapter presents detailed narratives of 10 complex, compound journey cases. Each of these cases provides the opportunity to examine, using a management innovation lens, what happens when organizations make efforts to improve their project management practice.

By examining these cases in detail, we tease out the dynamics of innovation journeys: the types of innovation events that were undertaken, who was involved, the triggers for action, and the underlying forces—both external and internal to the organization—that influenced the evolution of the innovation journey. Each of these case narratives concludes with interpretation of the journey, based on extant innovation theory discussed in Chapter 2, that explicitly examines the characteristics of an innovation event (intentional, new to locality, changes to organizational system, an improved way of working, anticipated benefits from innovation), the phase of the innovation journey (initiation and adoption or implementation, adaptation, diffusion, stabilization, routinization), reproducing conditions and other influencing factors (sponsorship, leadership, external triggers, acceptance/resistance).

Each of the case discussions is introduced with one quotation from a key informant that is representative of the cumulative attitudes of the organization's employees (including all levels of employees, up to C-level executives) toward the project management implementation.

Case 23 – Continuous Refinement of Best Practices

> "Project managers [are] often involve[d] in project management discussion and process formulation, they communicate with PMO to reflect current situation and propose their own advice." — Human Resources, Case 23

Based in China and operating nationally from Shanghai, this organization carries out work in the information technology (IT) sector, undertaking mainly customer-driven project work. The company originated as an entrepreneurial pioneering start-up

Table 6.1. Context of Case 23

Organizational Context	Cultural Context
National Chinese IT organization for software and financial processing solutions. Highly competitive and is state-owned.	The predominant culture in this organization is entrepreneurial, customer- and investor-focused; success and failure are both tolerated.

approximately 10 years before the research study. (For more details on this case, see the Appendix.) The key contextual variables influencing this organization's innovation journey are summarized in Table 6.1.

In 1999, the IT function of this organization recognized a need for formal project management to improve customer satisfaction and project control. It took what was considered a revolutionary action for it, and implemented ISO9001 to achieve formal planning, control, and demand-analysis. By 2004, the company had recognized that the goals of the first innovation had not been fully met. The need to further renovate its practice in order to provide a more formalized project management function and assurance of quality led to its working with a capability maturity model (CMM3). It also instituted and used a project management office (PMO). In 2005, this innovation journey was extended to include status reporting and scoring systems for projects, and it was further polished in 2007 and 2008 by bringing in a lessons learned database and a training program. This innovation journey is illustrated in Figure 6.1.

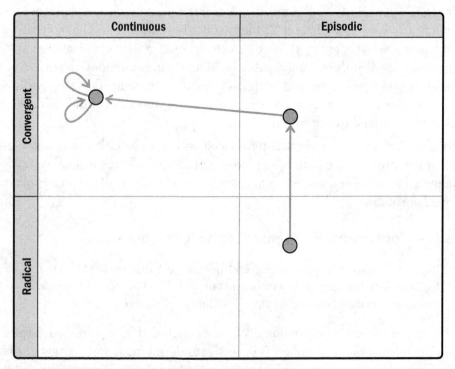

Figure 6.1. Compound innovation journey, Case 23

This organization innovated its project management in two major episodes: the first radically, using external best practice (ISO 9001); the second, building on to converge its practice by fixing a shortfall using a second external approach (CMM3). Subsequent innovations were then Continuous, aimed at refining practices in order to further converge them for maximum effect. Both tangible and intangible benefits were attributed to this journey, and the value trend of this organization was determined to be upward (+1), meaning that the investment to date was expected to continue to generate benefits to the organization. Each innovation event depicted in Figure 6.1 is described in Table 6.2 by date, innovation made, event type (based on Figure 3.2 plus the single-step innovation), and journey type (characterized in Figure 3.5).

Table 6.2. Timing and Type of Innovation Events for Case 23

Date	Intervention	Event Type	Journey Type
1999	ISO9001 to achieve formal planning and control	Punctuated (Episodic and Radical)	
			Reinforcing
2004	CMM3, a more formalized project management function and assurance of quality	Tectonic (Episodic and Convergent	
			Renovating
2005	Status reporting and scoring system	Persistent (Continuous and Convergent)	
			Polishing
2007	Lesson learned database	Persistent (Continuous and Convergent)	
			Polishing
2008	Training program	Persistent (Continuous and Convergent)	

Journey Dynamics

A Revolutionary Start to a Journey

The Episodic and Radical decision and subsequent action to implement ISO9001 in 1999 was a significant point in time for the Case 23 organization on its project management implementation journey. In an attempt to increase market share, this Punctuated event sought to put in place completely new project management practices across the entire organization.

Reinforcing the Journey (Punctuated to Tectonic Event)

Between 1999 and 2004, as the new practices were implemented, insufficiencies were exposed (such as resource constraints in 2000, and later a lack of focus on customer satisfaction). A second tectonic event in 2004 saw implementation of a new more formalized project management function and quality-assurance measures. The reinforcement of the original project management practices using a different approach—CMM3, a QA department, and quality-management initiatives—was an Episodic event, intended to help project managers control projects within the budget and schedule, and build customer focus (new solutions to resolve IT problems) in order to win the market.

Renovation Journey (Tectonic to Persistent Event)

As project management implementation became formally reinforced in the organization, project managers learned the techniques step by step. This was seen as favorable to the company, and "beneficial to their lives." In an attempt to measure its project management methods, a scoring system was implemented. Executives scored project managers according to the effectiveness of project implementation, and the project manager with the top ranking was named the winner. This event in the journey was a Continuous improvement to, and Convergent with, existing practices.

Polishing Journey (Series of Persistent Events)

In this phase of the journey, the PMO cooperated with the HR department to carry out project management training and professional project management authentication within the company. The PMO worked out plans with regard to the project management training requirements at the beginning of every year, and handed over the proposal to the HR manager to put into practice.

At the time of our data collection, the project management implementation was thought by the researchers to be well suited to the organization. Since it was a project-based organization, almost every employee in the company was involved in project management improvement.

Key Insights from Case 23 Journey

This innovation journey began with a decision to adopt a recognized Western standard management practice aimed at quality improvement. The organization's intention in adopting these measures was to improve its project management practice. The decision to implement ISO9000 standards came in response to external competitive pressures, and was made by the top levels of management. The changes to project management practices were quite extreme, were triggered by external market conditions, and came about as a result of a more global decision taken at the top levels of the organization. These decisions necessitated significant change to project management practices.

The second innovation event was another externally triggered effort to adopt external standards, this time CMM IT standards. The trigger for this event was the recognition of project management challenges not addressed by the introduction of ISO9000 quality standards. Again the organization entered into mimetic behavior, adopting externally set standards, and again the decision was made outside of the project management departments. However, this time the effort was made to more thoroughly embed project management practices within the organization by developing internal departments with responsibility for improving project management practices.

The next innovation event was driven by the internal champions who had recognized flaws in the practices adopted as part of ISO9000 and CMMM. This innovation event built on these newly implemented standards, but elaborated on reporting structures and focused on better use of existing tools. This part of the journey thus continued through a series of Convergent and Continuous innovation events, all of which built on the organization's existing project management model.

By the end of our data collection we could see that project management was firmly adopted in the work practices of this organization, with support at all levels of the organization. The organization had implemented Continuous improvement-type innovation cycles to maintain the fit of the project management model with changing requirements. By the time we collected information from this case, project management was recognized as an important work activity by all of the organization's stakeholders, and the necessity to continuously monitor and innovate in reaction to changes in the organizational context was well recognized across the organization. Project management, while well routinized and socialized within the processes and people of this organization, was still thought of as something that required creative thought and ongoing investment and learning if it was going to be maintained. This reflects the conceptual discussion in Chapter 2.

Case 25 – Evolving and Polishing a Diamond

> "The biggest effect is that somebody sat down and started to formulate a [company] project model. [Previously], people invented something again and again to the new projects. So we have started to create a uniform basis in the company." — Interviewee, Case 25

This organization is the largest IT public-sector provider in Denmark, with 60% of the market share. It undertakes mainly customer-driven project work. (For more details on this case, see the Appendix.) The key contextual variables influencing this organization's innovation journey are summarized in Table 6.3.

Table 6.3. Context of Case 25

Organizational Context	Cultural Context
The largest IT public-sector provider in Denmark, this organization has several international competitors. The current level of moderate competition is expected to increase.	The predominant culture in this organization is innovative and competitive. A respected view of project management exists within this organization, although the attitude is more combative to recent change. This organization's project managers have won awards.

In the mid-1980s this organization introduced the role of project management to complex work tasks in response to increasing complexity in its work projects. Project management processes were introduced in the early 1990s, and a formal PMO was created in the early 2000s. Certification began in 2002 as a way to improve project manager education and introduce a common conceptual framework. In 2003, new project managers were supported by mentors specific to the three different types of project managers then operative. The organization sought to increase improvements in its project management for one area of its business, and introduced a project management model in 2004. This was followed in 2004 by the formation of a knowledge sharing network to bring together the project management model and project management certification education. In 2007 the role of project director was created, and the director was made a member of the executive board. In that same year, certification was supported by specific mandatory training, project managers were PRINCE2 certified, and project managers won awards from professional associations. The project management model was extended, and a uniform management model for customer projects was developed that constitutes the foundation of Continuous improvement. This innovation journey is illustrated in Figure 6.2.

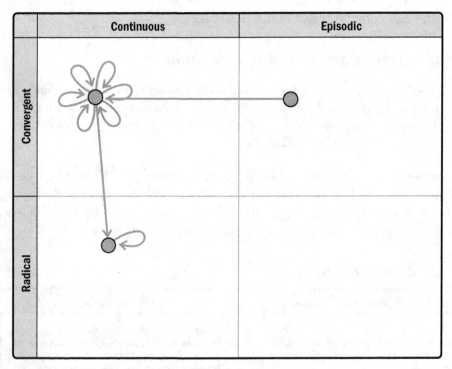

Figure 6.2. Compound innovation journey, Case 25

This organization was able to embrace and support each of the innovations to its project management journey. It started with continually converging to a system that was effective and efficient for it, polishing its practice with each innovation. At a critical point in its experience, it disseminated its practice more widely. These actions positioned this organization on a strong upward trend toward gaining value from project management innovation with tangible and intangible benefits. It has seen increases in capability through communication efficiencies, and greater competence through certification, which has resulted in larger contracts and professional recognition for its practices. Each innovation event depicted in Figure 6.2 is described in the following section.

Table 6.4. Timing and Type of Innovation Events for Case 25

Date	Intervention	Event Type	Journey Type
mid-1980s	Introduction of formalized project management within IT group	Tectonic (Episodic and Convergent)	Renovation
2000	PMO	Persistent Continuous and Convergent)	Polishing
2002	Certification of education IPMA	Persistent (Continuous and Convergent)	Polishing
2003	Introduction of mentoring of project managers	Persistent (Continuous and Convergent)	Polishing
2004	Project management model municipality reform model	Persistent (Continuous and Convergent)	Polishing
2004	Knowledge-sharing network to improve previous certification event	Persistent (Continuous and Convergent)	Polishing
2007	Client project model introduced	Persistent (Continuous and Convergent)	Polishing
2007	Mandatory training in PRINCE2	Persistent (Continuous and Convergent)	Integratory
2007	PRINCE2 organization-wide	Turbulent (Continuous and Radical)	Embedding
2007	Project director on board	Turbulent (Continuous and (Radical)	

Journey Dynamics

A Tectonic Event Starts the Journey

In the mid-1980s this organization formally introduced project management. The role of project managers was to work on complex tasks in response to increasing complexity in the organization's work projects, arising from higher market pressure and greater customer demands. Standard project management processes were used to develop methodical and generic practices across the workforce.

Renovation Journey (Tectonic to Persistent Event)

It was recognized that project management could be more formal, and so project management was given a supported upgrade when a PMO was created in the early 2000s. The PMO was intended to support employees to work with best practices consistently across the organization. Project management became more of a standardized discipline. Courses in project management were offered.

Polishing Journey (Series of Persistent Events)

Certification of project managers began in 2002 as a way to improve project manager education and introduce a common conceptual framework. In 2003, a mentor program was initiated to support new project managers. The mentors were specific to the three different types of project managers in this organization. The pace of improvements in project management was accelerated when the organization won a contract for a major program of 60 projects. This program required support that would increase project coordination and control to ensure completion of the projects within contracted deadlines. The organization's flat organizational structure, which included little administration, meant that there was a lot of unassisted leadership at the employee level. The organization introduced a project management model in 2004, seeking to increase improvements in its project management to cope with the challenges of managing an increased number of projects. This was followed in 2004 by the formation of a knowledge-sharing network to bring together the project management model and project management certification education. These changes led to high rates of customer satisfaction, cost reductions, and reported higher self-esteem in project teams as they saw that they had been successful in delivering project objectives. These achievements were recognized inside and outside the company.

Integratory Journey (Persistent to Turbulent Event)

The success of the polishing initiatives was recognized in 2007 when certification was further supported by the introduction of specific mandatory training: all project managers were to become PRINCE2 certified. This innovation to create a certificated workforce was put in place to ensure a more united and professional profile in relation to handling customers. PRINCE2 was chosen as the certification program to enhance focus on the models more than on the methods. Project managers were nominated and won awards from professional bodies. The project management model was extended to improve focus on business case and project charter activity. A uniform management model for customer projects was developed that constituted the foundation of Continuous improvement.

Embedding Journey (Turbulent to Turbulent Event)

Later in 2007, the existing role of project director was made a member of the executive board. This was a clear statement of the embedded status that project management had attained within this organization, and the organization-wide recognition of the importance of project management to the work of the organization.

Key Insights from Case 25 Journey

This organization began its project management innovation journey three decades ago, when its executive recognized that the central activity of the organization *was* project management, and reorganized to support this understanding. This recognition was an internally generated need driven by company management's efforts to address rapidly changing project environments, and it was attained through a structural revision and the introduction of the role of project management. The project management role descriptions were internally generated by workers, and for the next 20 years the company focused on refining and developing this nascent project management model. All employees were socialized to understand "how projects are done around here," and encouraged to contribute to efforts to improve the practice of project management. Project management tools, procedures, and infrastructure (PMO) were developed through a series of Continuous, Convergent, or polishing project management innovation events.

This organization was able to embrace and support each of the innovations that contributed to its project management journey. Its experience gives substance to the theoretical discussion on the importance of socialization, willingness to learn together based on trust, the importance of relationships, and secure identities. The company started with Continual Convergence toward a system that was effective and efficient for it, polishing its practice with each innovation. It based innovation on its own organizational learning—adopting some aspects of extant models but avoiding the "check-the-boxes" approach to measuring competency or performance in project management, in favor of innovations tailored to its particular practice of project management.

Recognizing the success to date of in-house project management development, and the growing complexity of the projects and programs the company was undertaking, the organization decided to adopt a more standardized project management approach based in PRINCE2 methods in order to simplify the hiring of new project managers and transferability of skillsets. Once PRINCE2 methods were well accepted in the project management departments, the PRINCE2 practices were disseminated more widely.

These actions placed this organization on an upward trend in terms of gaining value from project management innovation. The organization has seen increases in capability through communication efficiencies, and greater competence through certification, which has resulted in larger contracts as well as professional recognition for its practices. Our researchers saw that significant value had been generated by the careful, incremental approach this organization had taken toward the introduction and dissemination of project management practices and changes generated by its employees through a process of collaboration and learning. In particular, the company realized value in terms of employee satisfaction, customer satisfaction, and greater cross-project communication. The researchers on this case noted the importance of the common frame of reference that was fully adopted, and grew into the project management. Project managers expressed a multifaceted view of project management—one that includes well-developed tools and methods, as well as clearly defined roles for the project organization, combined with management focus on leadership rather than project control (Eskerod & Riis, 2009b).

The focus on shared learning, common language, internal buy-in and corporate capacity development demonstrated by this company gives additional support to innovation theories that stress the importance of providing space and time to allow for creativity, prolonged innovative efforts, and identity construction.

Case 34 – Aligning Us All, Except Where It Doesn't

> "With further improvements and wider acceptance of a structured [project management] methodology across the organization, potential value is enormous." — Project Manager, Case 34

Based in the UK and operating nationally and internationally, this university carries out work in a competitive education sector. (For more details on this case, see the Appendix.) The key contextual variables influencing this organization's innovation journey are summarized in Table 6.5.

This organization is very young in its project management innovation journey. Although project management has been present in this organization in some areas since the late 1990s, the latest organization-wide innovation is by far the most innovative.

Table 6.5. Context of Case 34

Organizational Context	Cultural Context
Working nationally and internationally in the UK educational sector, this organization experiences complex competition based on a number of factors such as price, resource, quality, and reputation.	The predominant culture in this organization is innovative, customer- and stakeholder-focused, but with a strong element of academic collegiality, values, and respect for academic freedom.

A proposal to adopt a single formal system (PRINCE2) in 2006 for managing significant projects across the entire organization was introduced by a new member of the senior management team, and was supported at the highest level of management. However, the approach was resisted in some areas because it ran counter to the academic culture. The implementation was introduced as a control mechanism, which, through best practice, was expected to help improve alignment of project work. Employees were expected to buy in and show compliance to the formal process. This innovation journey is illustrated in Figure 6.3.

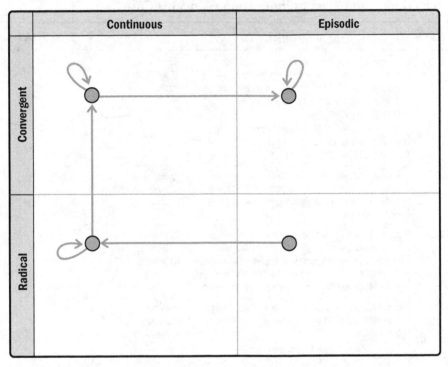

Figure 6.3. Compound innovation journey, Case 34

Although initially this innovation began with an Episodic and Radical event, it quickly became Convergent although still Radical. Attempts to integrate the approach across the organization amounted to a Turbulent event, which resulted in resistance. The innovation was not intended to disrupt culture but was expected to act as a Continuous and then Convergent change to practice. However, the change was harder to adopt in some areas of this organization than management had hoped, due to cultural issues, but it was continued to be seen within the organization's management as strategic alignment. The innovation journey brought some intangible benefits for this organization but the conflicting perceptions around the journey did not yield the potential value, seen in some areas, across the whole of this organization.

A subsequent intervention promoting the certification of PRINCE2 users for some areas of the organization underlined formal project management more firmly, while acknowledging it did not need to be implemented everywhere. The mandated use of PRINCE2 for the university's restructuring project sought further to underline the strategic use of project management to the whole organization. Each innovation event depicted in Figure 6.3 is described in the following section.

Table 6.6. Timing and Type of Innovation Events for Case 34

Date	Intervention	Event Type	Journey Type
2006	A newly recruited member of the senior management team, who came from a very senior position in the public sector, had a strong conviction of the positive effects of project management as a management innovation. As a result, the Special Student Experience (SSE) initiative was labeled a project in order to be managed as a project.	Punctuated (Episodic and Radical)	Embracing
2006	A sponsor, a senior academic, was appointed as director of the project with decision-making power and control over the project; reported directly to the vice chancellor.	Turbulent (Continuous and Radical)	Embedding
2006	A professional project manager (trained in project management, from the professional staff of the university's IT department) was appointed to manage the project, to the shock and disapproval of the project team members, who were mostly academic.	Turbulent (Continuous and Radical)	Integratory
2006	Introduction of project management method was promoted as almost a guarantee of the success of the projects. Formalization of project management using PRINCE2 across organization. Project manager began introducing best practices, mostly relying on her training in PRINCE2.	Persistent (Continuous and Convergent)	Polishing
2007	Professional project manager starts to try to implement project chartering process: significant resistance results. Project manager leaves project. Work completed following more collegial academic culture procedures.	Persistent (Continuous and Convergent)	Intervention
2008	PRINCE 2 certification promoted in some areas of organization.	Tectonic (Episodic and Convergent)	Fix
2010	University Level Restructuring Initiative is marked as a high-level priority and designated as a project. It is managed using the formal project management methodology PRINCE2.	Tectonic (Episodic and Convergent)	

Journey Dynamics

A Punctuated Start to the Journey

The recruitment of a senior-level manager into the senior management team from a high position in the public sector created a new perspective on project management for this organization. This manager had both experience and a positive view of project management as a management innovation. As a result, the organization's Special Student Experience (SSE) initiative was labeled as a project and managed using project management. This was a small revolutionary event for the university, in that projects and project management had not previously been formally acknowledged as relevant to university initiatives.

Embracing Journey (Punctuated to Turbulent Event)

The project management process introduced to manage the initial projects was further reinforced by management when it appointed a senior academic to the role of director of the project. This Radical appointment allowed the director decision-making power and control over the project, and a direct reporting line to the vice chancellor.

Embedding Journey (Turbulent to Turbulent Event)

A second radical step to further underline executive support for the adoption of formal project management within this organization was the appointment of a professionally trained project manager (from the IT department). This step was received with shock and disapproval by the project team members, who were mostly academic.

Integratory Journey (Turbulent to Persistent Event)

With the support of senior management, project management formalization using PRINCE2 was implemented across the organization. The project manager began introducing best practices, mostly relying on her training in PRINCE2, to create Continuous and Convergent adoption of PRINCE2.

Polishing Journey (Persistent Events)

The introduction of a project chartering process, designed to add Convergent improvement to the formalization, uncovered issues around adoption and acceptance not having occurred. In the face of this non-adoption the project manager left, and the work was completed without the use of PRINCE2 methods.

Intervention Journey (Persistent to Tectonic Event)

To underline that PRINCE2 was the formal methodology for project management, certification in PRINCE2 was introduced in some areas of operation. There was some administrative improvement with this Episodic action, but buy-in was not universal.

Fix Journey (Tectonic to Tectonic Event)

A high-level, high-priority university-wide restructuring initiative was designated as a project, and managed with PRINCE2 methods. This was a further Episodic event aimed at bringing Convergence to fix the perceptions around formalized project management practices by means of example.

Key Insights from Case 34

This case is a very interesting example of a Radical innovation event that resulted in only partial adoption because of the vested interests of a powerful cohort within the organization. In this case, PRINCE2 project management methods came into conflict with established academic culture. Trying to implement and enforce hierarchical reporting structures and procedures with clear deadlines and lines of accountability rapidly came into direct conflict with the collegial, collaborative, and deliberative culture of academics. In this case, the desire to "get things done" came into direct conflict with the desire to "do the right thing." This conflict and resistance was exacerbated by the lack of understanding of the academic culture by the new administrator and the PRINCE2-certified project manager who first attempted to manage the SSE project. If these two champions had more experience and understanding of how these practices were likely to clash with the academic culture and had planned for a slower conversion process, they might have been more successful. However, their attempt to quickly implement these practices so foreign to the academic culture led to rejection.

In this case, it is important to understand the role of the project management innovation champion in the innovation efforts. This individual came from a government background where PRINCE2 was accepted as the way to manage projects; indeed, it was so totally socialized and routinized in public administration that there would have been no reason for the new senior manager in this case—who had come from the public sector—to think carefully through the potential for resistance. Due to that preexisting perspective, and without a solid understanding of past practice or organizational culture in the new setting, this champion made a strong initial innovation intervention without paying any attention to the social dynamics. The manager was not sensitive to, and in fact overlooked, the cultural diversity between the two settings and the potential for resistance, including the perceived legitimacy around formalized project management.

The later stages of the implementation journey in Case 34 are also interesting. Having failed in their efforts to use the SSE project as a model for how to manage work at the institution, the PRINCE2 champions decided to increase the number of PRINCE2-certified project managers throughout the organization—believing that this would increase acceptance and decrease future resistance to PRINCE2 initiatives. Unfortunately, those chosen for training were members of the professional and technical staff throughout the university, and after they had completed their training, they found they had very little support from the academic administration to implement this way of working. Again this seems to indicate a lack of understanding on the part of management of who needed to be influenced to gain acceptance for this change in work practices, and the fundamental difference between organizational and academic approaches.

The final innovation event was another effort to showcase the effectiveness of PRINCE2 management methods by using them on another strategically important project—this time one with less academic involvement. The success of this project likely improved the status of PRINCE2 with many administrative groups at the university, but still did not have much effect on the academics. This left us wondering what the next step would be: would the administration recognize the importance of gaining the support of the academics, who constituted a crucial and powerful stakeholder group, to improve the success of its management innovation efforts? Or would it continue to attempt to marginalize this group and try to work around them?

Case 35 – Radical Change Followed by Effective Ongoing Refinement

"We have not only followed the government regulations, but we have been continuously establishing and innovating our own management system according to the company's development and the industry's situation." — Project Manager, Case 35

Based in Beijing, this very large national Chinese construction organization undertakes mainly customer-driven projects. (For more details on this case, see the Appendix.) The key contextual variables influencing this organization's innovation journey are summarized in Table 6.7.

Table 6.7. Context of Case 35

Organizational Context	Cultural Context
One of the top 20 national Chinese construction companies, this Beijing-based organization faces fierce competition. It is state-owned and is regarded as highly competitive.	The predominant culture in this organization is customer- and investor-focused. This organization has a heavy emphasis on project management implementation. Project management is respected within this organization. Operating within the Chinese cultural context means that workers have many more shared values, including a longer-term horizon, than Western workers. A shared commitment to a common goal is more easily obtained.

In 1995 this organization realized its capability and defined itself as a project-based organization. In a Revolutionary action, it adopted a full-implementation approach to project management, following world-wide best-practice methods. Researchers indicated that "project management was introduced by the company following the governmental regulations and laws." The company followed the standard approach, working to refine and polish its system in small ways to align with its own operational requirements. Its most recent innovation in this respect is its use of its nine years of practice to build an internal, case-based training program. The innovation journey is illustrated in Figure 6.4.

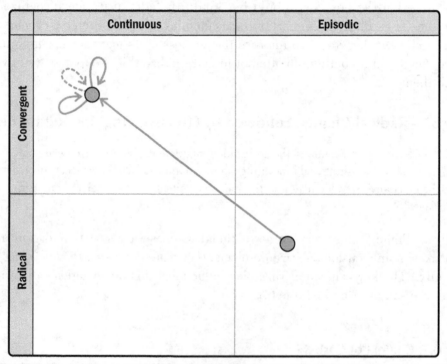

Figure 6.4. Compound innovation journey, Case 35

The cooperation and alignment of this project-based organization in adopting and refining the standard approach has been of great benefit to this organization. Due to its polishing innovations, the value that can be identified as an outcome of its project management initiatives is expected to continue to trend upward (Thomas & Mullaly, 2008). Each innovation event on this journey is described in some detail in the following section.

Table 6.8. Timing and Type of Innovation Events for Case 35

Date	Intervention	Event Type	Journey Type
1995	Organization defined itself as project-based organization per government requirement	Punctuated (Episodic and Radical)	Revolutionary
	Series of extensions and improvement of project management systems, including training	Persistent (Continuous and Convergent)	Polishing
	Series of extensions and improvement of project management systems including quality and safety controls	Persistent (Continuous and Convergent)	Polishing
2006	Implemented new training based on locally created cases, which acts as a "lessons learned" case book	Persistent (Continuous and Convergent)	

Journey Dynamics

A Punctuated Event Starts a Revolutionary Journey (Punctuated to Persistent Event)

This organization identified itself as a project-based organization and, motivated by government regulation and a need to be more competitive in the marketplace, adopted a full-implementation approach to project management following worldwide best-practice methods. This innovation toward formally managing work in terms of projects was entirely new to this organization, and resulted in a change to cultural and working practices throughout the organization.

Polishing Journey (Series of Persistent Events)

After the initial revolution, this organization sought to follow its successes by improving employee and organizational project management capability through a series of Continuous and Convergent innovations. Although this organization did not detail the set of Continuous Convergent innovations it implemented over the period 1995 to 2006, it created a fully mature project management system by continuously updating its processes and work practices. Study interviewees noted the variety of training techniques used, and the focus on improving quality for safety as well as quality for increased reputation. The latest innovation, in 2006, was the introduction of a training system based on organizational project case histories, thereby providing a lessons-learned component to the training experience.

Key Insights from Case 35

This organization began its innovation journey faced with the dual challenges of finding its way in a newly competitive private industry, and adapting to externally imposed Western-management practices. Almost everything about these adopted processes was new and foreign to all organization stakeholders. Their introduction to project management was truly both Episodic and Radical. However, starting the journey in this manner provided significant motivation for the organization to implement changes as effectively as possible, and then to make them work over time—a good example of socialization and collective learning.

The extreme external triggers made it relatively easy to direct the attention of the workforce and the executive to implement the necessary changes. As discussed in Chapter 2, when outside forces and threats create uncertainty and fear of consequences, implementation becomes the imperative. For this organization, the necessity to implement this innovation also created the focus, interest, and effort necessary to continually innovate, revise, and revisit its practices, to continue to make them fit into the organization's rapidly changing business environment. This company has continued to improve its project management practice through Continuous Convergent innovations aimed at perfecting the model it first introduced 20 years ago.

The role of the project champion is much less distinct in this case than in Case 34. External powers required the initial adoption of project management; after that was done, it became a collective organizational objective to use and improve these techniques. There was no key individual (identified to us) who introduced the innovation to this organization or who created an internal climate to encourage its implementation in this case. Rather, it appears to have been a regulated change that the organization accepted as important (see West's model of team integration, discussed in Chapter 2).

There may be a cultural component to the shape of this journey, as we did see similar pathways with other Chinese organizations. It seems that an extreme external trigger is necessary to start the innovation journey, but sustained commitment to improving practice is very much a central tenet of Chinese culture. As a result, the ongoing local interpretation of project management practices results in relatively frequent innovations. There may be another cultural influence as well, in the reporting aspect of this story that was given to our researchers. In the Chinese culture, recognizing individuals as being important to the process of innovation may not be an acceptable way to frame the story of an innovation. For this reason, we may not have gained full access to the social dynamics of the innovation journey in the Chinese case studies.

Case 43 – Playing Keep-up and Getting Buy-in

> "I've got some good project managers who follow due process in the right sort of format and utilize project management intelligently, and others who just take shortcuts and it's quite high maintenance to keep them on track." — Project Manager, Case 43

Operating regionally in Queensland, Australia, this organization carries out public-sector project work for the government. (For more details on this case, see the Appendix.) The key contextual variables influencing this organization's innovation journey are summarized in Table 6.9.

Table 6.9. Context of Case 43

Organizational Context	Cultural Context
A regional organization in Queensland, Australia working in the public sector. Although the competition for projects is low, there is a high level of competition with the private sector for resources (both staff and materials).	The predominant culture in this organization is innovative, with a focus on customers and stakeholders. Project management is recognized as central to the organization's existence, as success in projects is fundamental. A cooperative view of project management exists within this organization.

In the early 1990s, this organization recognized itself as a project-based organization that needed to support a variety of differently sized projects managed by a range of project management methods. It chose to innovate its practice by working to integrate the *PMBOK® Guide* approach with its own experiences. The organization thereby created its own methodology, in a process described as a "low-level revolution." This accumulation of its own and best practice is seen as Radical and Continuous within existing frameworks of practice. Later in the 1990s, a project management unit was created to support existing practice. Over the following years, evidence grew that improvements in estimation capability were needed to increase performance in project management, and in 2002 a tool was employed to fix this situation. By 2007 (the last sample date for this case), the increase in number and complexity of projects required further accumulative improvements to competency in project management, and mentoring was put in place to achieve this. This journey is depicted in Figure 6.5.

Only time will tell whether the promising initial innovation and project management unit, driven by some project employees, will continue to meet the newer requirements for project management caused by changes in project number and complexity. The fix in 2002 and the polishing adjustment in 2007 may have been in response to an initial insufficient innovation, which built on existing project management. The presence of reluctant adopters or the retreat from process in crisis situations in the empirical data could indicate that the innovation is not quite aligned to this organization's need. The organization may be on the right path, but the next investment will be a key indicator as to the ongoing suitability of its methods. The value this organization was determined to be gaining from project management is neutral/static.

Table 6.10. Timing and Type of Innovation Events for Case 43

Date	Intervention	Event Type	Journey Type
1990s	Recognized self as project-based organization	Turbulent	Integratory
1998/9	Project management unit	Persistent	Intervention
2002	Model project plus implemented	Tectonic	Renovation
2007	Consultant used to help with mentoring, rewards, staff retention	Persistent	

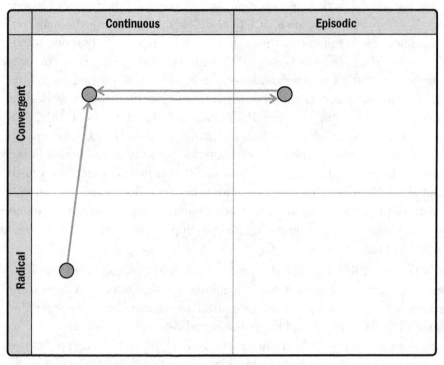

Figure 6.5. Compound innovation journey, Case 43

Journey Dynamics

A Turbulent Start to the Journey

In the early 1990s, this organization recognized itself as project-based and saw that it needed to support a variety of differently sized projects managed by a range of methods. It chose to innovate its practice by working to integrate the *PMBOK® Guide* approach with its own experiences, creating its own methodology, in a process described as a "low-level revolution."

Integratory Journey (Turbulent to Persistent Event)

The formation of a project management unit in the late 1990s took the Radical change of being a project-based organization and integrated it to normal working practice by creating an opportunity for Continuous Convergent supported actions.

Intervention Journey (Persistent to Tectonic Event)

A large formalization of project management in this organization was adopted in 2002, with support from directors, senior project managers, and project manager management. In a specific innovation Convergent with existing practices, the model, Project Plus, was implemented to improve performance, particularly in estimating time and budget. This led to high levels of customer and stakeholder satisfaction. Many projects were delivered on time, on budget, and with extremely high quality.

Renovation Journey (Tectonic to Persistent Event)

Further extensions to the formalized project management model were then used to look at increased capability in project management in response to staff losses and increased infrastructure demands. Consultants were brought in to help with mentoring, rewards, and staff retention. The implementation was put in place to support the use and understanding of the project management framework, and to increase project management capability during staff shortages.

The researcher saw value in the high rates of customer and stakeholder satisfaction, and in the fact that many projects were delivered on time, on budget and with extremely high quality. There was also evidence of improvements in risk management, coaching, and training, and in program management. Scope was managed to an increasing degree, resulting in measurably fewer incidences of scope creep in recent projects. In terms of organizational culture, it was felt that the whole organization had a stronger affinity for accountability and delivery after the changes had been implemented.

Key Insights from Case 43

This organization started with a central recognition of the importance of good project management practices to its operations, and decided to integrate standard project management "best practices"—as evidenced in the emerging bodies of knowledge— into its own processes. This integration, described as a "low-level revolution," was intended to create a single methodology that would be in part new to the organization, and would be suitable for its range of project sizes. Over a period of time, the organization continued to improve and adopt externally generated project management innovations. The organization's second innovation was to develop the infrastructure in the form of a PMO to support Continuous innovation in practices. Both of these early innovations were internally motivated in response to external conditions, but with the full involvement and interest of all internal project management resources. The vested interests of this particular group of internal actors created the group integration that was necessary to support collective action and learning. Based on emerging external professional discourse, standards and products were adopted to increase the perception of the legitimacy of these management innovations.

The next innovation event involved bringing in external consultants to help implement more formalized approaches to project management. This Episodic intervention was a fix aimed at improving customer satisfaction while containing scope creep. It was seen as successful, and was supported by a Convergent, Continuous innovation event that was aimed to increase project management capacity over the same or fewer project managers, by means of increased training in risk and program management, and the coaching of project managers. Some could see this last innovation as an attempt at work intensification that might result in resistance to the new methods, but at the time the research was conducted, there was no evidence that these efforts had been perceived this way. The support through mentoring for the new work systems that had been instituted is likely to illustrate an adoption of the process, and is the beginning of the standardization and routinized diffusion of work practice in the organization.

Case 47 – Best-in-Class Project Management with Disappointing Results

"This unit made a huge investment in project management a few years ago and is a success story within our entire organization for what they have accomplished in project management." — Senior management, Case 47

On the reason for the latest innovation: "The program was out of control . . ." — Senior management, Case 47

A multinational defense contractor based in the UK, this standalone project business unit is responsible for engineering projects and undertakes mainly customer- and product-driven project work. (For more details on this case, see the Appendix.) The key contextual variables influencing this organization's innovation journey are summarized in Table 6.11.

This work unit was formed in 1996, employing the project management practices of the established parent organization. By 1998, the project management of the unit was clearly ineffective. The project was overdue, and a revision of the work schedule was created. No changes to project management practices were implemented. Later, further schedule renegotiations occurred, along with some changes to project

Table 6.11. Context of Case 47

Organizational Context	Cultural Context
UK multinational engineering organization working in the aerospace defense sector with widely held ownership structure.	The predominant culture in this organization is customer- and stakeholder-focused. A complex relationship exists between this organization and clients, influenced by the perceived quality of project management practice within this organization. This organization has a strong engineering focus with a cooperative but dismissive view of project management. This attitude is coupled with a very strong perception that the organization does world-class project management.

management practice: for example, in 2002, an incremental delivery mechanism was put in place. Despite external reviews that advised management that a change in project management was required, only ineffective small incremental "polishing" innovations were put in place. In 2003 the customer and organization agreed to draw a line under existing issues and implement an earned value reporting approach to increase control. At the time of reporting, this innovation has apparently satisfied customer needs, although it has not addressed the previously identified project management issues. The key events in this journey are depicted in Figure 6.6.

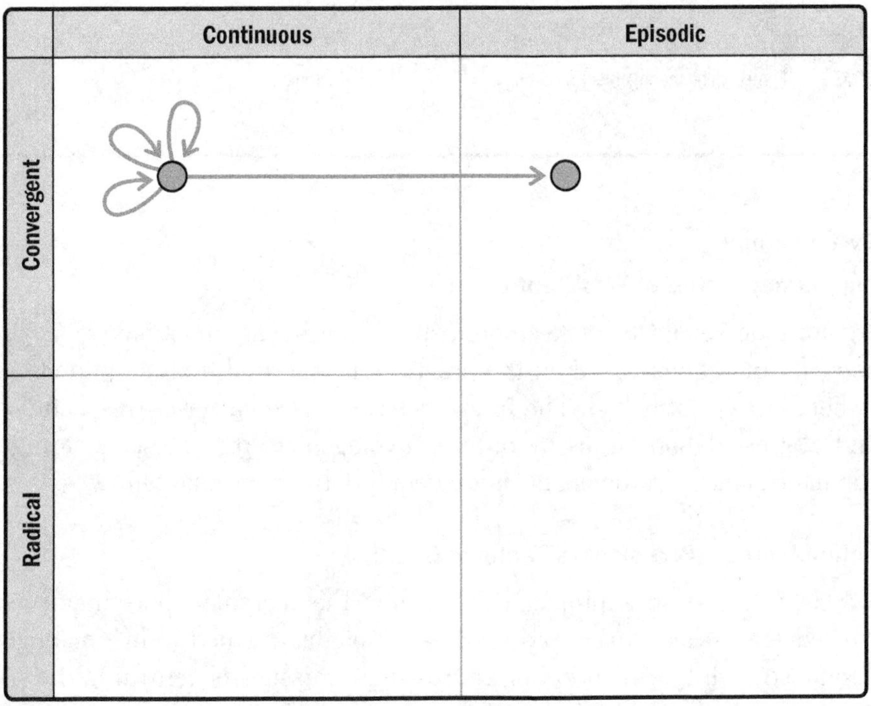

Figure 6.6 Compound innovation journey, Case 47

The perceived value trend of this case's innovation journey is downward (−1). It did not reflect any of the effective classes of innovation journey witnessed in other cases. The organization's early "polishing" actions did not address the underlying issues; in fact, they emphasized organizational confidence in its project management approach, despite solid evidence (external reviews) suggesting that it did not meet project needs. The isolated fix put in place as the latest innovation, although yielding tangible value, also did not address the existing issues in the management of the project. From the researchers' perspective, this organization requires a revolutionary change to its project management practice.

Table 6.12. Timing and Type of Innovation Events for Case 47

Date	Intervention	Event Type	Journey Type
1996	Adopting parent organization's methodologies	Persistent (Continuous and Convergent)	Polishing
1998	Work schedule management methods	Persistent (Continuous and Convergent)	Polishing
2002	Changes to management practices—incremental delivery mechanism	Persistent (Continuous and Convergent)	Polishing
2002	Further incremental improvement in project management practices	Persistent (Continuous and Convergent)	Intervention
2003	Earned value management reporting	Tectonic (Episodic and Convergent)	

Journey Dynamics

Polishing Journey (Series of Persistent Events)

This organization sought to make incremental Continuous and Convergent project management innovations based on the practices it inherited from its parent organization when it was established. The innovations addressed a series of schedule slippage and cost escalation issues by refining management practices, including work schedule management methods and incremental delivery mechanisms.

Intervention Journey (Persistent to Tectonic Event)

In 2003, in response to a project crisis, when the incremental refinements had not resolved the issues, an intervention was sought. Earned value management was introduced with the intention of addressing the issues of returning the project to schedule and budget. The innovation was intended to create more control and oversight of the project by introducing predictability. It was also intended to enable understanding around cause and effect in the schedule, and increase client perception of the project's being in control and manageable.

Key Insights from Case 47

Within the contractor company, the innovation journey that was studied in this case is held up as a great success. The project is now seen as exemplifying "good" or "best" practice throughout the parent organization. A prime outcome of the innovation journey is that the program is no longer under threat of closure. The company retained the business, and the project fell "below the radar" with the client. The relationship with the customer became much better. Planning disciplines were implemented. People working on the project appeared motivated and confident in both the product and the new processes. However, the actual tools and techniques that were focused on (earned value) had very little impact on the management of the project, as evidenced by the ongoing failure to meet either schedule or budget targets. This failure to improve project management practice, even with significant investment in consulting, training, and procedures, is likely attributable to the fact that the changes made paid only lip service to the prevalent problems in the organization. Many of these relate to the underlying motivations of the parties involved, and the dominant techno culture.

When the client's grievances with schedule slippage and other existing project management practices became too loud for the organization's management to ignore (or to overrule by proclaiming its project management prowess and reputation), the global organization chose to change the leadership of the unit. A new and highly respected manager from the parent national organization was sent to manage the unit in 2002. He began by implementing some Continuous Convergent management innovations, but when these did not satisfy the client, he convinced the head office that a substantial investment in management innovation was necessary. The decision was made to pay a prominent strategy management consulting firm a considerable sum to implement world-class earned value reporting (a technique specifically designed to ascertain how much has been spent for what activities, rather than to help manage schedules). The cachet of the consulting firm, the amount of money invested, and the reputation of this new manager all contributed to satisfy the client's concerns about schedule and delivery, and the contract was renewed.

The tangible value of the investment in earned value accounting in guaranteeing the renewal of this very large project contract was truly significant. However, the intangible value most often associated with such investments was missing. In addition, the value trend for project management in this organization was strongly negative. Not only was earned value not being managed appropriately, there was very little evidence of even the most basic of project management practices being consistently adhered to at the time this case study was collected (2006).

Careful analysis of this case is included in Brady and Maylor (2010), who discussed the social dynamics of investing in earned value as a signal of innovation and improvement. This article went as far to suggest that the company and the client were complicit in delivering legitimacy to the investment, while no discernible improvements were actually made to the practice of project management. The focus of this innovation is about being seen "to be acting quickly and doing something substantial," rather than revealing the actual issues and "doing the right thing." This seems clearly to have been an innovation journey that was never initiated with true intent to improve practice. In the beginning the company was socialized to believe in the superiority of its practices to the extent that, even in the face of strong evidence that these practices were failing it, it appears to have not critically examined or changed these practices. When the evidence (and customer dissatisfaction) became too great to ignore, the key players in the management of this organization deliberately engaged in behavior designed to improve the legitimacy of its practices, while not making a serious effort to improve practice. This case reinforces two aspects of innovation journeys: (1) implementation of innovation is difficult, and will be avoided unless the external pressures are great enough to outweigh the effort that will be required; and (2) where the identity of the key players is completely tied up in protecting practice image, it will be difficult for innovation to take root.

Case 52 – Buying into the Journey to Gain Value

> "I think it is great to work with projects, when I feel that it gives value for the company—whether it is a new system or a fall in working hours. It is great when the employee realizes how much [benefit] the projects have given them." — PM Management, Case 52

The engineering and logistics subunit of a major international pharmaceutical organization operating from Copenhagen, Denmark, undertakes mainly product-driven project work. (For more details on this case, see the Appendix.) The key contextual variables influencing this organization's innovation journey are summarized in Table 6.13.

Table 6.13. Context of Case 52

Organizational Context	Cultural Context
An international pharmaceutical organization based in Denmark with a widely held ownership structure. The Supply Operations & Engineering department is responsible for production and logistics projects, undertaking mainly product-driven project work.	The predominant culture in this organization is strongly professional with some silos of knowledge. A respected view of project management exists within the organization.

Under the view of a new director, this organization identified an insufficiency in its project management system in 2000. It attempted to fix its practice by implementing a new information system to measure and monitor resource usage. However, in 2002 this fix was superseded by a revolutionary change to project management practice governance and control, with the implementation of a PMO. In 2005, the PMO was extended across the organization in response to increased numbers of projects and resource demands; the changes coincided with an organization-wide definition of what would be considered a project versus an operational task. The final innovation studied was a further integration action to promote increasing efficiency in the existing functional methodology. The key events in this journey are depicted in Figure 6.7.

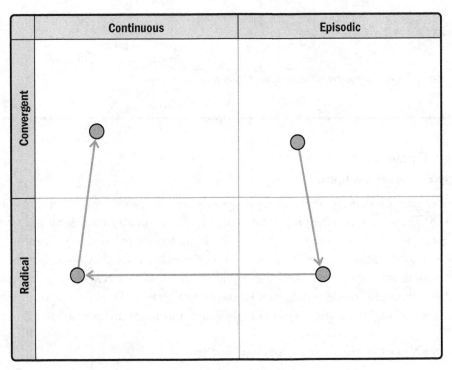

Figure 6.7. Compound innovation journey, Case 52

The initial innovation under new management was a fix to the existing system, which was then upgraded to a change to the working practices as they related to project management. The rollout of the method across the organization and refinement of the definition of what would be classified as a project was a Radical innovation: the organization was clearly building on existing frames of reference and experiences. The organization's final innovations were refinements intended to make efficiency gains, which at the time of data capture had not yet created tangible benefits, although the interventions had delivered many intangible benefits. The perceived trend for the value of project management in this organization was neutral: its practice met its current needs but was not perceived to be able to bring further value in its existing format. Each innovation event on this journey is described in detail in the following section.

Table 6.14. Timing and Type of Innovation Events for Case 52

Date	Intervention	Event Type	Journey Type
2000	System to measure and monitor resource usage	Tectonic (Episodic and Convergent)	
			Rejected fix
2002	PMO implemented: supersedes previous system	Punctuated (Episodic and Radical)	
			Embracing
2005	PMO adopted across organization	Turbulent (Continuous and Radical)	
			Integratory
2007	Refinements in the method to make efficiency gains	Persistent (Consistent and Convergent)	

Journey Dynamics

A Tectonic Start to the Journey

This organization experienced dramatic growth, and its project work had to become more efficient to speed up the project process. The situation was at times characterized as chaotic, with many changes in the projects, including many more requirements for the construction of the facilities. On review, the existing quality management system was deemed insufficient, and was divided into separate resource management systems and a tailor-made production management system. The organization started its journey by implementing a system to measure and monitor resource usage.

Rejected Fix Journey (Tectonic to Punctuated Event)

The organization appointed a new divisional director who picked up on the separate systems issue, and this led to the implementation of a PMO. The aim was to create an integrated system that would allow measurement of how resources were used for projects. This would permit the departments to be able to book resources with each other. The projects in the portfolio were generally on track and they had no serious complications or delays. There was virtually no project backlog. Also, the introduction of the PMO, and in particular a stage gating process, focused more senior management attention on projects during the whole life-cycle, from initiation to closeout and beyond, to benefits realization. This development also furthered the process of avoiding scope creep in the projects.

Embracing Journey (Punctuated to Turbulent Event)

A project management governance (PMG) group was formed to endorse the organization-wide (and thus Radical) use of the PMO. The PMG group mandated project documentation and assessed project charters and closeout reports. The PMO supported the project managers, the project management implementation, and competence development of the project managers. Competence development initiatives included networking days twice a year on a variety of topics.

Integratory Journey (Turbulent to Persistent Event)

Once the PMO activity was embraced across the organization, more focus was placed on project management, with the number of projects increasing and more resources being channeled into projects. In addition, more tasks were defined as projects. A period of integration occurred that continuously and convergently refined the methods to increase efficiency. The classification of work into different categories was abandoned, simplifying work into two types: projects and departmental activities. Improvements occurred to ensure that the right projects were done, and that sufficient resources and benefits were achieved.

Key Insights from Case 52

This innovation journey was particularly interesting. Dynamic growth required existing systems to be made more efficient. The lack of efficiency was seen as something that could be fixed through the application of an appropriate tool. The journey therefore began with an innovation event designed to fix problems experienced in the management of resource usage on projects. Not surprisingly, this very focused and specific innovation did not address all the issues faced by project managers in this organization—rather it was seen as an attempt to control and manage them. This resulted in resistance.

The inadequacy of this approach was soon recognized, and a more radical and widely scoped intervention was developed. In this intervention, infrastructure was successfully introduced to facilitate new ways of working and to support multi-project programs and portfolios. This effort explicitly addressed the need to set common goals that would facilitate group integration and commitment to management innovation. Based on the success of this model in parts of the organization, the next innovation was to increase the project management governance capability in the organization, and then to integrate this best practice into the rest of the organization.

Finally, the organization recognized that there were different kinds of projects within its organization. It refined its project management practices through a Continuous Convergent adaption innovation event that allowed project-appropriate standardization and reproduced conditions of working. At this point, the organization shared a common perception and common language of project management through the socialization and learning efforts undertaken. That shared perception and clear communication capability allowed it to collectively engage with project management refinements.

In this case, as in many of the others, there are some key contextual situations and individuals that prompt the socio-behavioral and political conditions conducive to innovation. In this case, the initial failed intervention focusing on control and reporting helped the organization become more open to including the project managers in future improvement efforts. At the same time, the hiring of a new director with ideas about how to improve project management provided the championship for the efforts to make a revolutionary change throughout the organization rather than acting on one part of the organization. The combination of extreme growth, failed innovation, and new championship created the readiness to radically change management practice. The initial success of the radical innovation allowed the project management sponsor to gain political support to implement governance and project management infrastructure in order to nurture the innovation and maintain a high degree of alignment between the project management innovations and other management practices. The role of the project management sponsor in reading the organizational readiness and requirements was what enabled a Radical Episodic intervention with mixed results to persist through to successful project management innovation.

Case 63 – A Path to Growth Then Collapse

> "Efficiency at implementing/delivering on projects has increased because of project management. Project management's contribution is growing as [the] company grows." — Executive, Case 63

The focus for this case was on the PMO of a Canadian energy-sector organization. The PMO was responsible for IT projects, undertaking mainly internally driven work. However, over the course of the study, the PMO extended its reach into

Table 6.15. Context of Case 63

Organizational Context	Cultural Context
A western Canadian energy-sector organization with a strong IT project division.	The predominant culture in this organization is one of growth and entrepreneurship.
Income-trust ownership structure within a competitive environment of rapid growth and unpredictable demand.	There are many lines of business that experience friendly and collaborative yet intense and complex competition, both internally and externally. A cooperative to respected view of project management exists within the organization.
	The organization is young and began as an entrepreneurial start-up with a very strong focus on financial controls above and before all else.

engineering and strategic projects. (For more details on this case, see the Appendix.) Key contextual variables influencing this organization's innovation journey are summarized in Table 6.15.

The vision of the CIO of this organization was to prove the concept of project management and to realize its value across the whole organization. This vision was implemented by means of the creation of a formal project management methodology and an IT PMO office in 2007/2008. A specific staff member was hired to manage this implementation, and through her personal style, marketing, and training, this was an extremely successful venture. Senior managers quickly came on board and strongly encouraged the use of project management throughout the organization. This innovation was a Radical move to implement what was proven in one area (Information Systems [IS]) across the organization. The perceived value trend for this organization was positive, demonstrating considerable intangible benefits at the completion of the original data collection period. However, the loss of the project management champion at a key stage in the development of the strategic PMO resulted in almost total abandonment of this initiative. This journey is illustrated in Figure 6.8. Each event in this journey is described in detail in the next section.

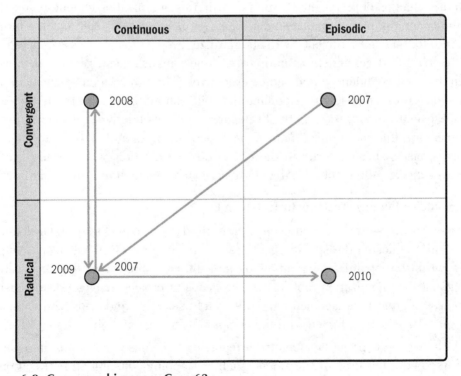

Figure 6.8. Compound journey, Case 63

Table 6.16. Timing and Type of Innovation Events for Case 63

Date	Intervention	Event Type	Journey Type
2007	Formal project management methodology	Tectonic (Episodic and Convergent)	Embedding
2007	Hired project management manager to set up IT PMO and changed project management reporting structure	Turbulent (Continuous and Radical)	Integrating
2008	Establishment of processes and training for project managers and managers on reporting and control	Persistent (Continuous and Convergent)	Integrating
2009	Corporate PMO to the whole organization	Turbulent (Continuous and Radical)	Failed roll out
2010	PMO killed	Punctuated (Episodic and Radical)	

Journey Dynamics

A Tectonic Start to the Journey

With the intention of preparing for high growth, this organization sought to "fix" the capability limit of project management. The specific goals were to provide a formal structure for managing projects with standardized, repeatable processes, as well as clear metrics for tracking status and costs. Project management gave IT increased credibility and confidence from senior executives. The project management implementation improved discipline, communication, commitment, accountability, and focus, especially among those in the IT department. The underlying vision was to use IT projects with formal project management methodologies and tools as a prototype for how projects should be run in the rest of the organization, which would lead to the next stage of rolling out formalized project management across the organization.

An Embedding Journey (Tectonic to Turbulent Event)

A manager to oversee project management was hired to set up the IT PMO. The founder of the PMO indicated the specific goals as: improving project management competency within the organization; improving and diffusing project management skills throughout the organization (not just in the heads of project managers); increasing awareness of project management; and, ultimately, selecting and prioritizing projects that were strategically aligned with the company's strategy and objectives.

A change to the project management reporting structure was also put into place, providing better resource management, such as stopping competition between projects for resources, especially on major capital projects and in light of the company's aggressive growth targets.

An Integratory Journey (Turbulent to Persistent Event)

Subsequent innovations continued to converge, with the lead taken by the development of the IT PMO. Project manager processes and training were established in addition to training for managers and senior managers on reporting and control, with the intention of ensuring that projects were on time, on budget, and met their mandates. The innovations were well executed and well championed through all levels of the organization.

An Integratory Journey (Persistent to Turbulent Event)

After the successes seen in the PMO, an additional, more radical innovation was proposed: to develop a corporate PMO accessible to the whole organization. The charter and status reports focused people's attention quickly to key issues. The COO also said that project management would help the company pursue long-term plans, adding value tactically by building understanding of human resource usage and increasing confidence in project delivery.

A Failed Rollout (Turbulent to Punctuated Event)

In a revolutionary change for this organization the IT PMO was devolved. This devolution was triggered by the impact of the introduction of the corporate PMO, and the extended leave of absence taken by the project management manager.

Key Insights from Case 63

This journey exemplifies two important features of many of the project management innovation journeys. The first is the critical role of the project champion in the success of the journey. In this case, the project consultant hired to implement some formal practices within this organization had the passion, energy, and reputation to first initiate and then lead a relatively rapid adoption of project management, beginning on a small scale and expanding to an organization-wide enterprise project management system in three years. Largely based on her tenacity and ability to get things done, she convinced an entire organization to change the way it thought about work effort. The importance of her role in supporting, encouraging, and maintaining organizational commitment to this initiative is highlighted by the fact that within three months of her departure, few remnants of the organizational project management infrastructure remained.

The individual capacity of the implementing project manager role to recognize potential sticking points and continually adapt both her approach and the nature of the innovation to the organization, and in particular to the strict-eyed accounting management of this organization, were critical to the success of the early phases of this innovation journey. Aligning the project management innovations to other ongoing needs and efforts in the organization, and building supportive coalitions within the power structure, allowed acceptance of policies and procedure many thought would never previously have fit in this organization. Early discussions with the critically important founding CEO, which built ties between fiscal governance and good project management practices, had an ongoing, and significant impact on the levels of influence this project manager had throughout the organization.

The second important feature relates to the fact that ongoing innovative effort requires substantial care and feeding. Without the constant attention of this highly respected individual, other managers quickly fell back into older patterns of behavior and work styles. Learning is a first step but if the efforts to routinize, socialize, and sustain the newly learned innovative practices are not maintained, the innovation is likely to wither. What remained in this organization at the end of the research were projects, a few project managers (although it did appear to be reverting to hiring external consulting project managers), and a very solid set of minimal project management practices, templates, and procedures that continued to be used in many areas of the organization following the departure of the project manager.

Case 72 – Revolution to Polishing

> "What we learned from the [project has] become the most valuable wealth of the company. We learned and practiced, and we then shared our experiences in the whole industry. And I believe more or less our experiences have also contributed to the relevant institutional reforms in the industry." — Senior Manager, Case 72

This construction organization operating from the Sichuan province of southwest China carries out projects in the energy sector. (For more details on this case, see the Appendix.) The key contextual variables influencing this organization's innovation journey are summarized in Table 6.17.

Table 6.17. Context of Case 72

Organizational Context	Cultural Context
State-owned national Chinese organization working in large-scale construction for the energy sector. There is little competitive pressure over the next 10 to 20 years for this organization.	The organization is project-oriented with a full project management implementation. A respected view of project management exists within this organization.

In 1984 an industry-wide management and administration reform occurred that was prompted by previous World Bank involvement and international collaboration with China. After setting up and registering in 1988–1990, the organization's initial challenge in 1991 was to integrate external project management practices to gain access to business funding. (In 1991 business funding was achieved, a World Bank loan was approved, and the organization used its industry-wide-management and administration in project management of its work. In 1995, a further World Bank loan was approved.)

After operating with this project management process, the capability and business of this organization grew. The subsequent challenge was to move from a single-project focus to working on multiple large-scale projects simultaneously. The company addressed this need by increasing its project managers' capability with training and certification. In 2005, it began a research project to investigate effective management systems and approaches. In 2006, the company issued guidelines for multi-project management and sought project management certification using project management training, and in 2007 it created an online training system organization-wide. This journey is illustrated in Figure 6.9.

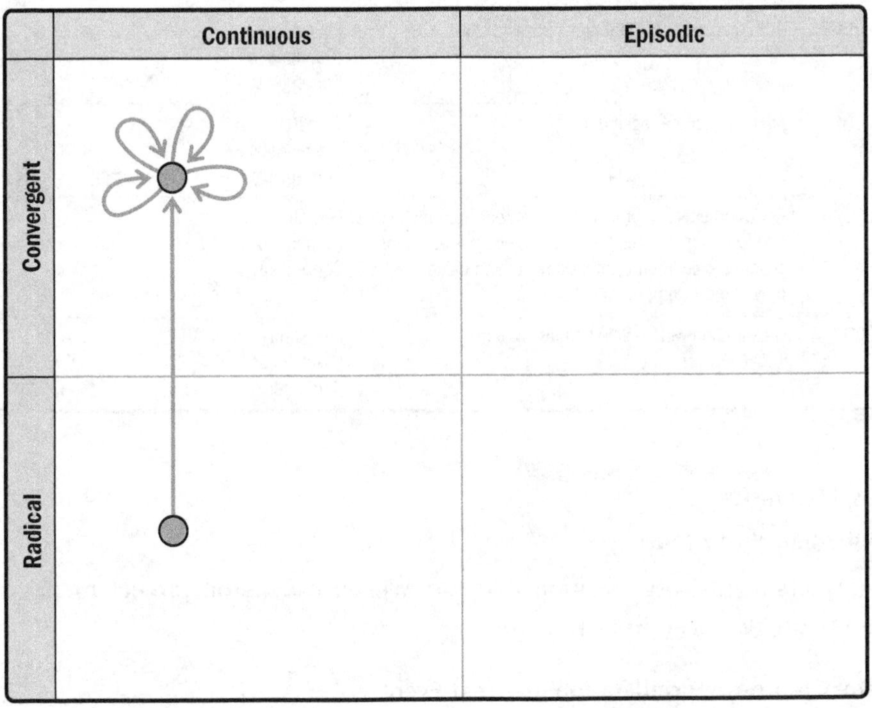

Figure 6.9. Compound innovation journey, Case 72

The organization adopted an industry-wide project management approach (put in place by following external practices), which it operated for approximately 14 years. The organization then examined what parts of that process were effective and sought to disseminate its findings by creating practice guidelines. This self-created mature practice model was then validated when the organization gained international certification based on its own in-house training; thus proven, the protocols were then disseminated throughout the organization. The organization gained many benefits and value from integrating and then polishing its practice; its value trended upward. This journey is illustrated in Figure 6.9 and described in Table 6.18. Each innovation event in this journey is described in detail in the following section.

Table 6.18. Timing and Type of Innovation Events for Case 72

Date	Intervention	Event Type	Journey Type
1988	Start of use of Western project management ideas	Turbulent (Continuous and Radical)	Integratory
1991	Extended project management to meet World Bank standards	Persistent (Continuous and Convergent)	Polishing
1995	Advanced management concepts and skills	Persistent (Continuous and Convergent)	Polishing
2001	Multi-project management	Persistent (Continuous and Convergent)	Polishing
2005/6	Reviewed effective project management approaches and issued guidelines for multi-project management, sought project management certification using project management training	Persistent (Continuous and Convergent)	Polishing
2007	Organization-wide online training system	Persistent (Continuous and Convergent)	

Journey Dynamics

A Turbulent Start to a Journey

At its formation, this organization adopted Western ideas on project management into its existing Chinese work practices.

Integratory Journey (Turbulent to Persistent Event)

The organization sought to extend its existing project management practice to incorporate international best practice to a level that would meet World Bank standards, and thereby secure funding for a large infrastructure project.

Polishing Journey (Series of Persistent Events)

In response to validation and feedback that its project management employed best practice and was considered mature, this organization sought to advanced its management concepts and skills so that it could undertake multi-project management.

The organization reviewed existing practices and external best practices, and made a number of Continuous and Convergent innovations.

Key Insights from Case 72

Similar to the other complex Chinese cases (23 and 35, and to many of the other Chinese cases in the larger dataset), project management was implemented in response to a fairly significant external trigger that mandated the form of the initial project management model. Subsequent Continuous Convergent innovation events reshaped and fitted the innovation to the needs of the organization. In this case, there was no evidence of resistance to the original Radical innovation, but there was evidence of significant ongoing efforts to tailor the practice over the long term. Standardization, routinization, and diffusion were not seen to be resisted within this organization's Chinese culture; however, attending to fit and organizational need allows the conditions for success to be created more easily. While the initially adopted model was mandated, the final adapted model likely bears little resemblance to this first step, due to diligent, ongoing efforts to improve the original model's fit with the organization's reality.

Case 75 – Searching for Solutions in a Garden of Possibilities

> "In examining the project management implementation at [Organization X], one is reminded of a large, well-established garden that has unfortunately become significantly overgrown, tangled, and broken down, even rotted in some places. One can see the original beauty, appreciate the careful selection and placement of the many different plants, and recognize the effort that went into balancing, juggling, and nurturing its various, sometimes conflicting needs: ultimately, creating an impressive showcase." — Researcher, Case 75

A North American multinational energy corporation based in Canada, this organization carries out work around the world. The focus of this case was on an award-winning IT PMO. (For more details on this case, see the Appendix.) The key contextual variables influencing this organization's innovation journey are summarized in Table 6.19.

Table 6.19. Context of Case 75

Organizational Context	Cultural Context
Canadian-based North American energy-sector multi-national. Operating in a competitive environment of rapid growth and unpredictable demand.	The predominant culture in this organization is in transition, with some silos of quite different cultures. It is recognized that project-based work is fundamental to this organization, but there is a mixed attitude to project management.

In the years 1999 to 2003, this organization set about refining a previously successful project management system in response to project failure issues. The trigger for its issues had been the retirement of its visionary project management leader, who had promoted and maintained a healthy PMO that acted as a center of excellence. The years following the loss of this individual saw a decline in the efficacy of the project management system due to lack of maintenance, lack of response to business changes, and lack of oversight in general. In 2004, the decline had reached a crisis point, and this was addressed with a Radical change in which the role of PMO was redefined from mentoring to control. This change did not completely solve the project issues this organization was facing. The next responses to the problems were a series of fixes that built on the control approach: in 2005, project governance was introduced that was in line with the current best practice trends in the project community at large; in 2006, a program management tier was added; and in 2008, process adherence was mandated. This journey is illustrated in Figure 6.10.

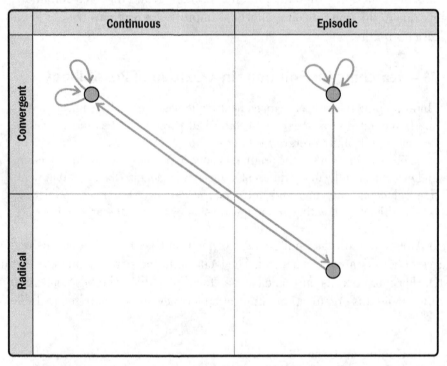

Figure 6.10. Compound innovation journey, Case 75

The trend for gaining value from project management in this organization was determined to be ineffective (−2): it was actually getting further from a valuable project management implementation as time progressed, and this was expected to continue with the journey pattern in operation. We interpret that its declining value was caused by two factors. First, it started innovating project management very successfully, so maintaining its successful practice would have been of value. Second, the organization lost its project management vision (its visionary retired), and subsequently decided that innovations were "done" (i.e., further maintenance and refinement stopped). Over time, fixes that were required but not picked up until too late necessitated Radical change. The change implemented at that point was one focusing on control. With project management perhaps no longer aligned with the remaining effective working practices, this produced a further devaluation of its project management implementation. What remained at the time of assessment was an approach to fix an implementation that no longer suited the organizational work process.

Table 6.20. Timing and Type of Innovation Events for Case 75

Date	Intervention	Event Type	Journey Type
1999	Formal project management process — Center of Excellence PMO	Punctuated (Episodic and Radical)	Revolutionary
2000	Templates	Persistent (Continuous and Convergent)	Polishing
2000	Mentoring	Persistent (Continuous and Convergent)	Polishing
2001	Benefits realization	Persistent (Continuous and Convergent)	Rejected implementation
2004	Control PMO	Punctuated (Episodic and Radical)	Reinforcing journey
2005	Project governance, portfolio managers	Tectonic (Episodic and Convergent)	Quick fix
2006	Program management	Tectonic (Episodic and Convergent)	Quick fix
2008	Mandated adherence to standards	Tectonic (Episodic and Convergent)	

Journey Dynamics

A Revolutionary Journey (Punctuated to Persistent Event)

In response to concerns over the organization's ability to deliver on critical Year 2000 IT projects, the initial innovation event for this organization was the hiring of a recently retired project management expert to create a Center of Excellence PMO. Designed to support the formal project management processes of this organization, the PMO grew under this individual's strong leadership. The leader recognized that the organization tended to rely on external project managers to lead most of its projects. This meant that even as nominal head of project management, he would have no real authority over these external resources, who would be most focused on delivering on their contractual requirements. In order to develop some consistency of practice, he needed these external resources to voluntarily agree to follow the project management practices he designed. The only way to gain their support and increase acceptance of the project management guidelines was to design them in ways that supported the efforts of these external project managers and helped them successfully deliver their projects rather than focus on developing a system of enforcement and control.

Polishing Journey (Series of Persistent Events)

The project management champion began by creating a set of project management templates to be used on all projects. His next intervention was to implement training, lunch-and-learn, and mentoring activities to help project managers understand how the templates were to be used. This series of Continuous and Convergent innovations was aimed at introducing and refining project management practices in response to project failure issues. These innovations were intended to improve on existing practices, converging methodology and processes in order to regain efficiencies by means of the use of refined templates, mentoring, and benefits realization. When the practices were fully implemented, the project management champion completed one last Continuous Convergent innovation event by implementing a benefits realization project for the PMO initiative. This initiative showed significant tangible and intangible benefits to the organization for the money invested in project management to date.

At this point, the leader returned to his retirement, and those left in the organization believed that they had completed all the project management they would ever need. There were no efforts to refine the templates or to train or mentor new people on their use. While the tools existed and it was suggested to new project managers that they use them, project management as it had been began to wither away.

A New Journey: A Rejected Implementation (Persistent to Punctuated Event)

When the project management process no longer seemed to be delivering benefits, and projects were again late and over budget on a regular basis, management decided to attempt to recapture the previous benefits the organization had received from the supported PMO implementation. This time they decided to introduce a control PMO instead. The purpose of the control PMO was not to support the execution of projects, but to execute projects through imposed management practices, regular audit activity, and the like. For this organization, redefining the role of the PMO from mentor to control was a revolutionizing event. Existing project management personnel were not totally on board with this change, and were not consulted, as management felt they were part of the problem. A manager with no industry or project management experience was hired to head up this unit.

Reinforcing Journey (Punctuated to Tectonic Event)

The project management issues were not immediately resolved by the control PMO innovation, and increased project governance in the form of Information Technology Infrastructure Library (a foundation set up to ensure good Information Technology infrastructure practices were followed) audit requirements were implemented to further bring the organization's project management practices in line with current project management trends.

Fixing Journey (Series of Tectonic Events)

The change to more highly controlled project management still did not resolve the organization's issues. The next management decision was the introduction of portfolio managers and program management to ensure stronger oversight of projects and reinforce control and governance. The organization also implemented a program of mandatory adherence to standards, in an attempt to bring all projects and project management in line. Most of this new management came either from outside project management or outside the organization. Few of the new portfolio managers had project management experience—it was not seen as a requirement for this important management role.

Key Insights from Case 75

This case may be most reasonably examined as two innovation journeys.

The first journey was highly successful, with a gentle hand on the tiller keeping changes relevant and effective. Recognizing the implementation of project management as a change to existing management practice that required buy-in from various levels in the organization and outside, the project management champion considered the social dynamics of innovation by including room for learning, routinizing, and socializing activities in all of his interventions. He started by supporting those who needed to do the work by providing a service to the project personnel. Then he branched out to show the value of the initiative in harder terms to the management levels, in an attempt to gain buy-in to the cultural change and continued investment in support activities and training. This journey ended with the retirement of the champion, an award-winning project management implementation, and a well-satisfied organization with definite evidence of the tangible and intangible benefits from its investment, but no understanding of any need for ongoing investment to sustain the benefits from the innovation journey traveled to date.

The second journey was unsuccessful at the time of writing, with a plan being forced through in an attempt to realize the benefits of a standardized approach focusing on control and measurement. The implementation was put in place to improve project performance and enforce adherence to procedures and processes. This second innovation effort seems to have ignored the cultural and learning elements of more successful innovation journeys—including the organization's own first journey.

Each successive investment in control and management (not project management, as few of the new managers actually had any project management training) added significant overhead and cost to the management of projects, but showed little evidence of actually improving the organization's capacity for managing projects.

The significant role of the first project management champion was crucial in delivering credibility to organizational practices, and in creating an environment for learning and innovation in which project managers were more likely to support the management innovations. This individual had the expertise to be credible in talking to project managers about how to improve practice, he was capable of learning and adapting best practice to fit organizational needs, and he was trusted by both project managers and upper managers to accomplish the implementation of management innovation.

The leader of the control PMO was a manager who came to the energy company with experience at a large bank. She had no experience in managing information technology portfolios or a PMO. As an outsider, she had no established networks within the organization from which to garner support. She needed to be seen to be doing the right thing quickly to solve the project problems, and chose to do this by adopting industry standards. By tying her innovation efforts to the standard setters, such as PMI and ITIL, she attempted to gain credibility and was able to show reasonable external legitimacy for her actions. However, having no project management experience seriously decreased her legitimacy with the internal and external project management staff. She failed to build on the earlier innovation journey, and indeed ignored its powerful results, creating some serious grounds for resistance from the staff.

Clearly, this journey was not complete during the time of our study, and whether the increased focus on control and conformance realized value in this organization was not known at the time of writing.

Chapter Summary

Management innovation implementation occurs as a result of actions of individuals and groups taken in a specific context, based in time and space. This chapter provided the detailed narratives of 10 complex compound journey cases in order to help the reader develop an awareness of the contextual factors, trigger events, innovation events, outcomes, and journeys these organizations engaged in as they pursued their efforts to improve project management practice. By examining these cases in detail we explored the dynamics of innovation journeys; what type of innovation events were undertaken; who was involved; the triggers for action; and the underlying forces both external and internal to the organization that influenced the evolution of the innovation journeys. Each of these case descriptions concluded with key insights from each journey based on extant innovation theory.

Each of these journeys was unique. And yet, elements of each journey will resonate with experienced practitioners and researchers. There are also commonalities, and there is much to be learned from by looking across these 10 cases. Chapter 7 is a cross-case comparison and analysis of these 10 complex journeys, flagging the similarities and differences among these cases. This provides a potent starting point for developing a deeper understanding of the journeys, and increasing our capacity to theorize their nature, as we will do in Chapter 8.

Chapter 7

Cross-case Analysis
of Complex Journeys

In Chapter 5 we considered what was done in the name of project management innovation and the context around it for each of 10 complex innovation journeys. In this chapter, we compare and contrast these journeys. This analysis allows us to explore, in a much more general sense, what the project management innovation journeys looked like from their beginnings, through development, up until the point at which our data capture ended. Attending to the 10 complex case journeys together and in comparison to each other allows the investigation of common and conflicting factors about project management innovation.

The analysis presented in this chapter considers the progression of innovations: it allows us to identify when an innovation journey begins, the stages through which it goes, and how to recognize when it ends. We consider the social and power relationships within the innovations: Who was involved in leading and sponsoring the innovation? What motivated the intention to innovate? How did that motivation change in relation to journey experiences? We also comment on the success and value delivered to the organizations by the various forms of innovation journeys they undertook.

Innovation Journeys

Summarizing the 10 complex and detailed journeys into a single table (Table 7.1) allowed us to begin to investigate the progression of project management in terms of management innovation over time.

Although all 10 journeys had more than four innovation events, some of them were more complex than others when duration, number of innovations, and types of change were considered. Our research approach was to consider innovation in project management as a series of innovation events (interventions). Based on that perspective, we saw that some organizations innovated continuously over a long period of time (e.g., Cases 23, 35, 43, 47, 52, 72, and 75 had all been innovating project management for more than 12 years), whereas some organizations (Cases 34 and 63) engaged in numerous innovation events but were relatively recently active in their innovation.

In Table 7.1 we illustrate these 10 complex journeys from start to end. The color and date of the block represents each innovation event in the cases' innovation journeys: Persistent events are represented with blue; Tectonic events with yellow; Punctuated events with green; and Turbulent events with red. Where the year is not specified (i.e., in Case 35), we have represented the time passage with an ellipse (...).

Table 7.1. Complex Project Management Innovation Journeys With Events by Date

Case Number										
23	1999	2003	2005	2007	2008					
25	1985	2000	2002	2003	2004	2004	2007	2007	2007	2007
34	2006	2006	2006	2006	2007	2008	2008			
35	1995	...	...	2006						
43	1995	1998	2002	2007						
47	1996	1998	2002	2002	2003					
52	2000	2002	2005	2007						
63	2007	2007	2008	2009	2010					
72	1988	1991	1995	2001	2005	2007				
75	1999	2000	2000	2001	2003	2004	2005	2006	2008	

It is worth noting that while the time based on calendar date when innovations were made in these cases is perhaps relevant to why an organization might innovate (i.e., it provides historical socio-economic context), what is more important in studying the process of innovation is the relative timing of interventions made. We are, for example, interested in the higher rate of incidence of Radical and Episodic events at the start of journeys rather than those seen toward the end and, similarly, the increased use of Continuous and Convergent innovation events nearer the end of the journeys than the beginnings. It is also highly interesting to investigate what the introduction of an Episodic innovation partway through a journey means for an innovation journey. We discuss this in depth next.

Start of the Journey

We can see that four of the 10 case organizations in our data set started their journeys with a Punctuated innovation (green), showing that they began with a Radical and Episodic intervention. This type of revolutionary change affects both the way the organization works and what it does, resulting in dramatic and organization-wide changes to its project management practice. Such changes may be implemented in response to external pressures, such as government regulation or funding body requirements (e.g., Case 35), or external events may require revolutionary action (e.g., Y2K preparation led to the initial innovation of a project management center of excellence in Case 75). There may be external/internal combinations, such as mergers and new management (e.g., Cases 23, 34, and the second intervention for Case 52, which was the start of the successful part of its project management innovation). In rare cases this type of revolutionary intervention could comprise a highly creative and novel *invention*; however, it is more likely to be an *innovation*.

Three other journeys (Cases 25, 52, 63) began their project management innovation journeys as part of large-scale, Episodic efforts to improve project management practices by converging practices in single initiatives. This constituted a Tectonic (yellow) intervention. These fixes were seen as successful—in which the journey either continued with a rollout to the wider organization (Case 63) or led to polishing (Case 25)—or as unsuccessful (as in Case 52, where the realization of the failure allowed the organization to restart its journey with a revolutionary invention). In both Cases 52 and 63, the organization did not get "stuck" in an unsuccessful fix; the intervention was perceived as inappropriate and a further, less Convergent, and more Radical innovation was implemented.

Two other organizations (Cases 43 and 72) started with a Radical, organization-level initiative (red), aimed at building on existing practices. Although adopting this change widely was a Turbulent intervention for the organization, the approach was known within the organization and was a continuation of an existing development.

Our analysis shows that nine of the 10 cases in the current study supported the findings of Thomas et al. (2002), who suggested that investment in project management is usually triggered by some sort of immediate need to radically revise an organization's project management practice. Only one of these organizations started with a continuous Convergent (blue) innovation, building in a Persistent manner on practices for managing projects that already existed in their organizations. This organization, Case 47, had a complex customer relationship where analysis has shown that both the organization and the customer were "complicit" (see a discussion of this case in Brady & Maylor, 2010) in allowing underperforming project management practices to be maintained over some time, and where even after a fix intervention, problematic project management practices remained and the value delivered from these interventions was actually negative. This finding, that external triggers cause organizations to initiate Radical innovations, is in contrast to our earlier description of the 48 journeys, where the tendency to start with a Persistent (blue) innovation was more common in more recent innovators, and in those for whom Continuous and Convergent (blue) interventions made up the sole investment in project management. This apparent growing use of Persistent interventions could be attributed to the increasing tendency of organizations to see project management as a tool and commodity, and to adopt legitimized approaches to project management that are now widely available from professional associations and consultants: these were not as prevalent in earlier years.

Middle to End of the Journey

Organizations refining and polishing their project management implementation undertake a series of Persistent (blue) innovations that are intended to continuously converge their practices. The anticipated benefits of these innovations are increases in efficiency and reputation. This type of polishing works well when the interventions are aligned with the organization's needs, and the foundations of the most recent Episodic or Radical (or both) intervention aligns with organizational operations and strategy (Cases 23, 25, 35, and 72 are good examples of this). The persistent cycling of Case 47 may provide an example of unmet needs.

Organizations with innovations that are Tectonic (Episodic and Convergent— i.e., in the yellow quadrant) sometimes enter a cycle of "fixing" actions. These organizations are typically seeking to reproduce effective project management conditions, and when they fail to do so with each new intervention, they try another. Fixes work well if they address the needs of the organization; however, as these episodes of intervention are convergent with existing practices, they do not have the ability to create change if the fundamentals of project management are no longer suitable for the organization. If the organization does not detect this failure, and the diffusion, stabilization, and routinization sought by these cycling organizations, whether it be in Tectonic (e.g., Case 75) or Persistent (e.g., Case 47) interventions, is not being achieved, then the organization is not likely to gain the anticipated benefits they expect from their interventions—or from their innovation journey overall.

The movement from one innovation to the next provides insight into the degree of success anticipated from the intervention. The Turbulent interventions for organizations requiring an organizational-level rollout are particularly illustrative. Cases 25, 34, 52, and 63 all moved into a Turbulent innovation event. Case 25 successfully integrated its well-adapted practice across the organization. Case 63 also integrated its practice across the organization, but in that case, the enterprise-wide rollout was not successfully embedded in organizational practice before the project management champion went on maternity leave, and without her strong leadership and sponsorship, the rollout was ultimately unsuccessful.

Two other promising innovation rollouts for new project management practices in Cases 34 and 52 had different outcomes. Case 34 ran into adoption resistance, due to a clash of cultures within different organizational staff (a clear case of lack of intergroup safety and integration). In Case 52, by contrast, attention was paid to ensuring that all organizational participants understood the benefits to be gained from the organization-wide adoption of the new practice, and these benefits were realized.

We also note in this analysis that within a process of change, it is not easy to define the boundaries of a journey. As we saw in the detailed description of these journeys in the last chapter, one case (75) appeared to have already engaged in a second journey, another (25) could have been seen as having two journeys, but the intention and anticipated benefits of the journeys overlapped sufficiently that the two journeys could be considered the same journey, and two more (Cases 52 and 63) appeared be on the point of starting a second journey at the end of the data capture period. Case 75 appeared to have engaged in a successful journey—developing a "center of excellence" PMO—but let it fall into disarray; it then decided to implement a control-oriented PMO that had not yet delivered project practice improvement or value at the end of the study. Case 25 began a successful journey to innovate its own project management practice, and completed it successfully, and then decided to institute PRINCE2 to achieve some standardization and make it easier to hire project managers. In this case, it is hard to say whether this was simply a continuation of the evolution of the project management practice, or a new journey. However, because the new PRINCE2 practices were socialized into the organization and integrated with the existing practices, which were not rejected, we believe that it was another step on this organization's journey, rather than a new journey. Case 52 appears to have had a false start, in that its original innovation was rejected, but then the organization went on to have a successful innovation journey that delivered significant ongoing benefits.

Finally, at the end of the original data collection efforts in 2008, Case 63 appeared to be one of the most successful project management implementation journeys, culminating in the development of an enterprise-wide project management office. However, in updating this case (between 2008 and 2011) we learned that efforts to embed this change in project management practice across the organization had failed and the enterprise-wide project management office had been disbanded. The increased discipline and workload for middle management in managing all projects in a rigorous way, combined with the lack of a politically savvy replacement for the original manager, created resistance to the initiative. It was judged as requiring too much "overhead" and the project management initiative failed.

This raises for us an important question of how we know when an innovation journey has been completed and can be judged as to its efficacy. The start and end of any innovation journey is an artificial construct depending on both the memories and judgment of participants, and the timing of data collection. Without the follow-up data collection on this case, it would have remained one of our most successful cases. This highlights the efficacy of our detailed case-based method in helping us to examine the complex dynamics of innovation across organizations.

Some organizations were clearly not at the ends of their journeys when the data collection ended. At the end of the period during which the data was collected, eight of the 10 cases (five in a Persistent innovation phase and three in a Tectonic phase) presented as being in a phase of convergence—varying only in the pace of the changes they made. They were either polishing their practices with Continuous Convergent change, or were periodically innovating practice to maintain convergence with existing practice.

Two cases (one with a Turbulent intervention and one with a Punctuated intervention) ended up in a phase of more Radical change. Despite this common outcome, they could not have been in more different places when the study concluded. Case 63 was possibly at the beginning of a new journey after the failure of a previous innovation. Case 25 was radically embedding its polished success—bringing it into the mainstream for the first time by including project management representation on the organization's board. This different experience underlines the need for contextual data. In order to ensure that the interpretation of innovation events reflects the actuality of the event, the context of the situation must be considered. It is not enough to merely code the innovation events: without the context, there is a serious risk that the type of innovation event will not offer enough information without context to assess the impact, motivation, triggers, and action taken. Sense-making requires that the interpretation of innovation events represents the reality of the event. The reasons for the need for a Radical change in Cases 25 and 63 were substantially different, illustrating the operation and importance of equifinality in these innovation journeys. It is not enough to know the type of innovation event (Persistent or Tectonic, etc.) to understand the socio-behavioral and political activity that either supported or resisted the intervention. Without being able to situate the event within its context, triggers, and key players, we cannot examine the dynamics or process of change involved in innovating, nor make reasonable predictions about the success of future interventions.

Innovation Triggers, Intentions, and Outcomes

Innovation is partly characterized by intentionality, and includes an expectation that benefits will arise from the intervention that will not only meet the intention but go beyond it. By examining the triggers, the intentions at the outset of the innovation journey, and the outcomes and benefits that were realized, we can make assertions about the process and success of the journey overall, and make sense of the results of the journeys. The interleaved nature of an innovation event (as shown in Figure 2.6) becomes apparent in this analysis. The outcomes of previous events and the cultural, economic, and organizational environment combine with a specific trigger and lead toward a contextual choice in setting the next intervention action and goal. Table 7.2 summarizes the triggers involved in establishing the intent around the entire innovation journey for each of our 10 detailed cases, and the benefits and a perceived trend of value from its innovation journey (details of how this trend was derived and the benefits identified can be found in Thomas & Mullaly, 2008).

Table 7.2. Triggers, Intentions, and Outcomes for Innovation Journeys

	Background to Intervention Trigger	Intentions for Innovation Journey	Outcome of Innovation		
			Value Trend	Tangible Value	Intangible Value
23	1999: Increased market share, need to control budget and schedule 2004: Need to improve quality 2005: Need to increase effectiveness of current practices 2007 and 2008: Need for systematic procedure to improve employee performance	• To improve customer satisfaction in terms of quality of deliverables and to facilitate less-experienced project managers to control projects within budget and on schedule • To start, increased market share; at the end, improving employee performance	Positive (1)	Some (2)	Some (2)
25	1990s: Formalize project management 2000: Upgrade of formalizing project management requires support 2002: Increase in workload, speed up initial training of new employees 2003: Improve effectiveness 2004: Improve flexibility and effectiveness—create a model with methods 2004: Use learned knowledge better 2007: Desire to use models, not methods 2007: United and professional approach with customers 2007: Spread the good work 2007: Underline importance of project management	• To cope with the challenges of managing a program of projects • Starting with standardizing methods and practices; ending with underlining the importance of project management in the organization	Strong positive (2)	Some (2)	Some (2)

Continued

Table 7.2. Triggers, Intentions, and Outcomes for Innovation Journeys *(Continued)*

	Background to Intervention Trigger	Intentions for Innovation Journey	Outcome of Innovation		
			Value Trend	Tangible Value	Intangible Value
34	2006: Vision in senior executive of project management as a management innovation 2006: Projects to become focal point 2006: Professional management of projects 2006: Formalization of project management approach 2007: Address resistance by formalizing commitment 2008: Project management to be formally adopted 2010: Project management practice to converge	• To facilitate formal control, visibility, and promotion of a series of interlinked projects • Starting with a vision for project management in the future; ending with implementing a project using the vision	Neutral (0)	None (0)	Some (2)
35	1995: Government regulatory requirements Up to 2006: Improve employee and organizational project management capability	• Starting with adopting project management to meet government regulation; ending with improving employee and organizational capability	Strong positive (2)	Most (3)	Most (3)
43	1990s: Recognition that project management is a central part of organizational function 1998/99: Employee-driven needs 2002: Address scope creep 2007: Increase project capacity and project management capability for reluctant adopters	• To provide support for use and understanding of a project management framework • Starting with an employee-driven improvement in project management capability, ending with need for further project management capability	Neutral (0)	None (0)	Some (2)

Table 7.2. Triggers, Intentions, and Outcomes for Innovation Journeys *(Continued)*

	Background to Intervention Trigger	Intentions for Innovation Journey	Outcome of Innovation		
			Value Trend	Tangible Value	Intangible Value
47	1996: Organization created; adopted parent organization's practices 1998–2002: Schedule slippage, cost escalations, etc. 2003: Increase customer control	• To increase client perception of project control and management • Starting with signs of project failure and ending with need to gain customer confidence	Negative (−1)	Most (3)	Few (1)
52	2000: Dramatic growth highlights need for efficiency 2002: Resource system issues, new divisional director 2005: Desire to roll out successful model 2007: Increase effectiveness for different project types	• To strengthen interaction (on projects) • Starting with a need to be more efficient to meet dramatic growth and ending with improving efficiency for different kinds of projects	Neutral (0)	None (0)	Some (2)
63	2007: Prepare for high growth 2007: Maximize use of project management for increasing capability 2008: Increase usage of process 2009: Get projects focused to add tactical value 2010: Loss of leadership and champion	• To prove the concept of and value of project management within IS and ultimately move PMO out of IS and become an organizational shared service. Specifically, to formalize project management structure and processes and as such improve project management competency within the organization. • Starting as increasing capability as a preparation to meet high growth, ending with changing implementation to reflect loss of the champion	Positive (1)	None (0)	Most (3)

Continued

Table 7.2. Triggers, Intentions, and Outcomes for Innovation Journeys *(Continued)*

	Background to Intervention Trigger	Intentions for Innovation Journey	Outcome of Innovation		
			Value Trend	Tangible Value	Intangible Value
72	1988: Company founded 1991: Desire to tap into international funding 1995: Do more of what is effective 2001: Manage multi-projects 2005/6: Increase effectiveness 2007: Use learned knowledge	• To rise to the challenge of managing multi-giant projects • Starting on the formation of the company with the project management implementation; ending with effectively using and learning from experiences	Positive (1)	Some (2)	Most (3)
75	1999: Coming Y2K IT projects 2000: Gain consistency and efficiency 2000: Ensure correct use of templates 2001: Review of value 2004: Development and mentoring stopped, benefits vanish 2005: Reinforce project management process and create benefits again 2006: Create benefits, process not being followed 2008: Process not being followed	• To improve project performance and enforce adherence to procedures and processes • Starting with ability to handle a range of Y2K projects through a benefits realization exercise; ending with needing process to be followed via mandated action	Negative (−2)	Some (2)	Few (1)

Triggers

The intention to innovate can be triggered by either internal requirements or external drivers. In these 10 cases, most innovations started with an external trigger or a combination of internal and external triggers. Initially, looking at triggers for all events in these 10 journeys, there is a suggestion that the majority were in fact triggered by internal pressures. Further investigation of the trigger for the initial project management improvement, showed in all cases except bar one (Case 52) that the cases started their innovation journeys because of external triggers, such as regulation, much-larger-than-usual projects that required more strategic attention, or failure to meet customer expectations. These cases then moved on to being triggered by internal factors. Only Case 47 was driven by external factors throughout its entire innovation journey. In Case 75, where there could be seen to be two journeys over the period of the study, the initial innovation journey was triggered by a need to be able to manage a large number of Y2K projects, and the second journey was triggered by the board's dissatisfaction with project management results.

Triggers that arise throughout the innovation journey reflect the outcomes of previous intervention events, as well as the environment in and around the organization. This means that there may be both internal and external triggers at times as the journey proceeds. The movement to internal triggers shadows the generalized movement from Radical interventions toward Persistent interventions, where the focus is an internally driven movement to make the best of the methods or models already implemented. It would appear that the nature of the triggers may also reflect the falling off of senior executive support, and the shift of responsibility for the championship of project management improvement to internal departments after the initial urgency of the external trigger is removed. As we know from the literature, external triggers related to competition and customers develop significant urgency that motivates implementation but does not provide space for creativity in innovation. The organizations that said "We have to do this" (i.e., due to government regulation or "because projects are our whole business") rapidly adopted existing work packages labeled as standards or "best practice" project management, and then spent years making it fit with their organizational needs through ongoing Continuous Convergent changes to the base model. Other organizations that continuously worked on improving their project management practice may have been able to create space for creativity and socialization over time, using more participative and creative learning processes. Organizations that were wrapped up in their own business pressures and simply sought an immediate fix to the current problem were the most likely to attempt to implement a packaged solution, drawing legitimacy from its success in other jurisdictions (see, for example, Cases 47 and 34).

Intentions

Of these 10 cases, three (23, 35, and 47) innovation journeys were intended to address customer or sponsor needs, seven (25, 34, 35, 43, 52, 63, and 72) were intended to expand capability, and two (34 and 75) were intended to increase control. Preliminary results of additional research work (Thomas & George, 2012) indicates that four categories of motivation exist for project management implementations. These are: (1) satisfaction; (2) efficiency; (3) power and control; and (4) legitimacy. Motivations and intentions for innovations can be multiple; for instance, Case 47 sought increased customer satisfaction, but perhaps more specifically wanted to legitimize its practice, Case 25 was concerned with satisfaction as well as power and control, while Case 75 was most concerned with achieving power and control, but was also interesting in improving efficiency. As we have mentioned in our discussion of triggers, the interleaved nature of previous outcomes and current situations sets the tone of intention both in the choice of action and the anticipated benefits.

Stakeholders in all 10 cases described to researchers an intended or anticipated benefit from implementing their interventions. Even Case 35, where the researcher did not list anticipated benefits in the report (the quote reads that the innovation implementation "appears to have been a regulated change that the organization accepted as important") illustrates that organization's ability to respond to, adopt, cooperate with, and ultimately adapt to a strong external trigger. In other words, it is not that this organization did not experience benefits (the Appendix clearly shows that it experienced a lot of them), but the anticipated benefit was extremely closely tied to the trigger: i.e., this organization met government regulations, and therefore was government-approved.

Outcomes

Innovation is characterized in part by having an anticipated benefit. The triggers and intentions we have discussed clearly indicate anticipated outcomes. In addition to experiencing some of the anticipated and intended outcomes of the innovation, the case organizations also experienced a range of other benefits (unintended outcomes)—some were intangible (such as meeting strategic objectives, and improving corporate culture, human resources, and reputation) and some (although fewer) were tangible (such as cost savings, customer retention, revenue increases, and reduced write-offs and rework).

Most of these multiple-innovation organizations had a higher than-average level of maturity compared to the rest of the cases in the sample, and also experienced tangible and/or intangible benefits. This may indicate the value of ongoing improvement in project management practices. However, there are a number of seemingly anomalous organizations in this group that bear further investigation.

Four of these organizations were assessed as "neutral" in terms of value trend, indicating that something was going on in these organizations that made it difficult for the researchers to assess the likely impact of the final project management implementation. Examining the case studies further, we see that the last project management innovation in these cases was implemented in the year prior to the year in which the data was collected. Thus, it may have been too early in the innovation process for researchers to assess the full impact of the final intervention in the study at the time of their reports.

Two of these multiple-innovation organizations were assessed as having a negative value trend after their final investment in project management. This seems anomalous until the case data is examined in greater detail. In one of the UK cases (47), the last project management innovation was an investment in consulting assistance that was intended to implement earned-value management tools in order to placate the client on a large and difficult contract. The goal was to get the contract renewed. The investment was made for legitimacy reasons, rather than actually to improve project management practice, and no improvement in project management was evident. However, the contract was renewed, and so the investment in earned value consultants returned a significant tangible benefit and some intangible benefits with respect to reputation. In one of the Canadian cases (75), after a very well received and beneficial series of project management innovations, the original project sponsor retired and the new manager responsible for project management made some significant organizational changes (Radical innovations). These changes required the introduction of additional levels of management (portfolio and program managers), and the new managers did not achieve their objectives. Here, organizations that had made numerous investments in project management chose as their next innovation an action that actually had a detrimental impact on the practice of project management.

Studying these cases intervention by intervention, it is possible to see how the outcomes (both intended and unintended) of one intervention, whether positive or negative, may trigger a subsequent intervention, thereby creating an overall profile of benefits, both anticipated and not. For example, Case 52 introduced an innovation to strengthen interaction between clients and staff, and among staff on projects. However, realizing that the first intervention did not result in the efficiency gains they had expected, they adapted their practices around resources so that they could receive efficiency benefits with their second intervention. Now having developed a model that worked, they rolled it out as their third intervention. Although this model did deliver effective project management, it needed to be refined a further time (a fourth intervention) in response to the different project types that the organization had undertaken. In other words, in order to provide the necessary flexibility to create real effectiveness, this organization gained improved corporate culture and attained its strategic objectives; these were valuable benefits in addition to the strengthened interaction that was originally anticipated.

In cases where the anticipated benefit was not met at all, as in Case 34, we saw that other benefits were still achieved, and that the anticipated and intended benefits were altered using feedback from previous outcomes, and new expectations were set. In Case 34, when only one group of employees adopted the innovation, this fact was actually embraced and developed, so that the non-adoption was in practice accepted. Strategically, of course this may create a change in the ongoing innovation journey, but one hopes that the affected organization will learn from past outcomes and alter future intervention implementation accordingly.

Sociopolitical Factors and Behaviors

Our consideration of the impact of sociopolitical factors and behaviors on the cases we examined includes: exploration of culture (including country, organizational culture, and attitude to project management); the behaviors and actions of those directly involved in the interventions and the innovation journey, as well as the leadership (key players) and sponsorship for the innovation; and the alignment of the project management implementation with the strategic direction of the organization. These factors all play a role in the success or failure of implementation journeys. Table 7.3 assesses our 10 cases with respect to these dimensions.

Culture (Country, Organizational Culture, and Attitude to Project Management)

As we have previously noted, the context of the case organization is needed in order to make sense of the project management innovation events made. For the 10 cases we are considering in detail, we present (in Table 7.3) organizational culture statements from collected data, market competition from market analysis data arising from the research of Thomas & Mullaly (2008), and a country cultural analysis from the work of Hofstede (2001, 2010). While we recognize the critiques of Hofstede's research (see, for example, McSweeney, 2002), we also recognize the value (as set out in Chapman, 1997) of using a recognizable shorthand for providing brief insights into the impact a country's culture may have on the socialization and routinization necessary for integrating group responses to project implementation.

Table 7.3. Cases' Country and Organizational Cultures

Country	Case Number	Country Culture					Market Competition	Organizational Culture
		Power Distance (PDI)	Individualism versus Collectivism (IDV)	Masculinity versus Femininity (MAS)	Uncertainty Avoidance (UAI)	Long-Term Orientation (LTO)		
Australia	43	36	90	61	51	31	Moderate	Innovative, customer- and stakeholder-focused
Canada	63	39	80	52	48	23	Moderate	Growth and entrepreneurship
Canada	75	39	80	52	48	23	Moderate	Customer- and Investor-focused
China	23	80	20	66	30	118	Very High	Entrepreneurial, customer- and investor-focused
China	35	80	20	66	30	118	High	Customer- and investor-focused
China	72	80	20	66	30	118	High	Customer- and investor-focused
Denmark	25	18	74	16	23	46	Moderate	Innovative and competitive
Denmark	52	18	74	16	23	46	Moderate	Strongly professional, with some silos of knowledge
UK	34	35	89	66	35	25	High	Innovative, customer- and stakeholder-focused
UK	47	35	89	66	35	25	n/a	Customer- and stakeholder-focused

Country Culture

The culture of countries can be differentiated on six dimensions (Hofstede, 2001; Hofstede, Hofstede, & Minkov, 2010), including Hofstede's original five dimensions of Power Distance (PDI), Individualism versus Collectivism (IDV), Masculinity versus Femininity (MAS), Uncertainty Avoidance (UAI), and Long Term Orientation (LTO), plus the additional category of Indulgence versus Restraint (IVR). As "Culture only exists by comparison. The country scores on the dimensions are relative— societies are compared to other societies. Without making a comparison a country score is meaningless" (Hofstede et al., 2010). The scores as such do not tell us all there is to know about the distinguishing differences from one country to another, but they do provide some contextual information that proves useful insight into some of the innovation dynamics.

For our 10 cases of interest, a few dimensions of differentiation across countries are evident from Hofstede's measures. China's culture has a much higher ranking on power distance (indicating a stronger reverence for authority and hierarchy), collectivism (impetus to work to a common or shared goal), and a long-term focus (content to make investments today for pay off in the future) than any of the other countries. Differences on these scales may account for our Chinese organizations' lack of resistance to often sudden and dramatic changes to work practices, as well as the commitment to continue to seek improvements to make the change work within the organization. Denmark is another interesting example, in that it has a higher ranking on the MAS scale for Femininity (attention to people and relationships) and a middle-term focus (LTO) which might explain the Danish cases' focus on collaborative learning and ongoing long-term investment in improving locally developed practice, while the more masculine and short-term-focused countries seemed more task driven and likely to throw out a project management model in the face of difficulty or a potentially better solution in order to deal with short-term financial quarterly results. On the uncertainty avoidance scale, all the countries in our sample exhibit relatively high uncertainty tolerance. Combining this score with the countries' scores on individualism versus collectivism seems to indicate that the Chinese deal with uncertainty through entrepreneurial adaptability, while the British and Danish tend to reflect individual curiosity.

Comparing the three cases in China with the two in the UK shows that the implementation journeys of all five organizations involved Persistent innovations, but those of the Chinese organizations were more likely to result in continuous improvement embedded in practice; those in the British organizations were less likely to result in the desired improvements, and were more likely to be rejected during future innovation efforts. If we examine the country culture scores, we could intuit that the difference in scores on Individualism versus Collectivity (IDV) scale may have something to do with the readiness with which the Chinese organizations were able to embed and routinize standards into practice for the good of the corporation, while the British organizations experienced more resistance to standardized practice. The country culture score relating to long-term orientation indicates that once a Chinese organization has adopted an approach, it is more likely to persevere in adapting to create benefits over the long term, in contrast to the shorter-term focus of the organizations in the UK, Canada, and Australia. The latter countries typically anticipate the realization of benefits within a much shorter time frame than the Chinese, if they are going to continue with an intervention. We have not explored this topic in detail, but we did see the need to mention it here: it became obvious to us in exploring our 10 cases that at least some of the success of certain implementations was attributable to the organization's having selected an innovation type that best fit with the culture of the people expected to accept the innovation. We leave more in-depth exploration of the impact of national culture on innovation journeys for future research.

Organizational Culture

Most of the 10 detailed cases reported a customer- and stakeholder-focused organizational culture, while several others reported innovative or entrepreneurial cultures. This was true even for some of the organizations operating in regulated economies such as China, and aligned with country culture scales and reported market competition. Most of these organizations saw their cultures as responsive and future-looking. This type of future-looking culture supports the triggers and intentions of meeting customer satisfaction. Clearly, in a culture framed by customer satisfaction and entrepreneurial attitudes, a deficit in customer satisfaction would provide external pressure and uncertainty that would trigger action. We do not have enough data to assess whether this observed relation between customer orientation and sensitivity to external triggers holds in all cases, but we suggest that it has face validity based in this data and in that presented in Thomas and Mullaly (2008), and that it should be explored further. "The organizational culture of our case organizations has been shown to be a factor in driving value from project management" (Thomas & Mullaly, 2008, pp. 287–333). Organizational culture is likely to impact both the triggers and intent of project management implementations. Planned innovations should also take into account how organizational members are most likely to accept and be motivated by change.

Attitude to Project Management

For each case we also have a researcher assessment of the organization's attitude toward project management. Table 7.4 shows that the attitude to project management ranges from Respected through Cooperative to Dismissive and Combative across these organizations. As might have been expected, in cases where the attitude toward project management was Respected and/or Cooperative (23, 35, 43, 52, 63, and 72), project champions faced less resistance and received more enthusiastic support and participation than in cases (34, 47, and 75) where Dismissive or Combative attitudes reigned (at least in some segments of the organizational population). The detailed descriptions of these 10 cases suggests that a recognition of these attitudes (as in the early journey of Case 75) helped the project management champion to design an implementation that would meet the organization's needs within the constraints of attitude and climate, and that ignorance of or assuming away these attitudes led to implementation efforts that faced severe resistance (as in Case 34). In Case 47, the attitude to project management was both cooperative and dismissive, in that the management and organizational members firmly believed that they practiced "world-class" project management, despite significant evidence to the contrary, and so implemented ineffectual Continuous Convergent improvements when required, until they were forced to invest in a major "fix" to satisfy client concerns. Even after this fix, the attitude to project management remained dismissive: no real value was expected from the fix. Case 25 provides a counter example, where deep respect for project management at all levels of the organization grew out of continuous Convergent innovation events at the departmental level, to the point where the last innovation event was to add a project management representative to the board. Clearly the attitude toward project management in the organization (and across groups in the organization) needs to be taken into consideration when planning project management innovations.

Table 7.4. Socio-Political and Behavioral Factors Related to the Adoption of Project Management Innovation

Case Number	Country	Key Players	Attitude to Project Management	Sponsorship	Research Perceived Alignment
23	China	Organization-wide. Project managers, the PMO, and HR department.	Respected	Executives and project managers	This is a project-based organization, almost every person in the company was involved in the project management improvement.
25	Denmark	Company project model from grass roots experience. Project managers win awards. PMO. Project director on executive board.	Respected to Combative	Top management team	Common frame of reference knowledge sharing, high quality, customer satisfaction

Continued

Table 7.4. Socio-Political and Behavioral Factors Related to the Adoption of Project Management Innovation *(Continued)*

Case Number	Country	Key Players	Attitude to Project Management	Sponsorship	Research Perceived Alignment
34	UK	Administrative employees. Senior management team.	Combative	Senior academic/ vice chancellor's office	Customer satisfaction, alignment of project business case with university's strategy better formulation
35	China	"The company," because of government regulations and laws. No key person— internal climate to encourage implementation.	Respected	Senior management, governmental regulation	Capability matches customer, subcontractor, and supplier expectations.
43	Australia	Project managers in a "low-level revolution." Project manager management unit. External consultants.	Cooperative	n/a	Project management is central to the organization's existence; if they don't deliver successful projects they will no longer exist. Only partial implementation exists.
47	UK	Perceptions of parent organization and client organization. Implementation by one senior manager and senior management. Management consulting firm.	Cooperative to Dismissive	Senior management	They are happy with what they have in place. There does not appear to be a fit between what the parent organization and the case study organization management tell us about the practice of project management in this case and the actual observed practice and attitudes toward project management.

Table 7.4. Socio-Political and Behavioral Factors Related to the Adoption of Project Management Innovation *(Continued)*

Case Number	Country	Key Players	Attitude to Project Management	Sponsorship	Research Perceived Alignment
52	Denmark	Director. Control PMO. Project Management Governance group.	Respected	Head of the PMO, the divisional director and the project management governance group	High
63	Canada	CIO. Manager for Project Management. IT PMO. Senior management.	Cooperative, Respected	Senior management, especially CIO, then COO.	Fits strategy, formal but grounded.
72	China	Senior management. Project managers.	Respected	Governmental regulation	
75	Canada	Visionary mentor initially. Support PMO. Management only no employee consultation. Non project manager in charge on control PMO.	Cooperative, Dismissive	Mostly at PMO level initially, then senior management devolved back to manager level.	By last innovation not aligned with strategy

Key Players

The social side of project management implementation is extremely important to its success. Thomas and Mullaly noted that "the role of seniority and experience has a significant role on many implementations" (2008, p. 356). This was particularly true for organizations where "expertise was developed and cultivated within the organization" (Thomas & Mullaly, 2008). There are three key groups of players in any project management implementation. The first is the executive sponsorship, the second is the individual or group champions, and the third is the group responsible for the practice of carrying out the project management (the practitioners and managers of project management). Each of these groups will be discussed next. It should be noted that in some cases executive sponsors or project personnel play the role of champions.

Sponsorship

Executive sponsorship is particularly evident in early innovation events triggered by external pressures, as would be expected from the innovation literature discussed in Chapter 2. The urgency involved in externally generated crises—such as that surrounding the Y2K initiatives that triggered Case 75's innovation journey, or the need for World Bank funding that triggered the journey of Case 35—results in significant executive attention and support. Executive sponsorship is also very strong where the project management innovation is an agenda item for a new executive trying to make a name in a new organization, as was true in Cases 34 and 63. Executive support is largely absent or passive in innovation events that build from earlier innovations through Continuous Convergent events, or which are led by project management groups that are outside the purview of executives. The most successful of our project management innovation journeys seem to be those triggered by external events with the attendant executive support to both initiate Radical innovations and provide ongoing support through continuous improvement activities that are designed to embed the changes into organizational practice over the long term. Case 35 is a good example of this, and the early part of the journey of Case 75 seemed to be on track to this sort of success as well. However, once executive support was withdrawn in Case 75, the implementation effort (though continuing through another department-led standardization effort) withered and grew ineffective, leading to another externally triggered intervention.

Even with strong sponsorship of an innovation, the cultural attitude impacts the successful implementation as discussed above. The cultural attitudes of Cases 35 and 72 led to cooperative action and developed a respected project management implementation that was widely used within the organization. This arose from the need to accept and embrace innovation that was triggered by governmental regulation. The cultural aspects of Case 34 also impacted that organization's innovation, but in that case the implementation was rejected by some of the organization's employees, leading to quite a different journey. Although Case 34 saw sponsorship in the form of a management directive from a new executive who was making his mark, the organization had a divided cultural attitude toward project management and the innovation was not accepted universally.

Project Implementers: Champions, Leaders, and Teams

In some cases there is a clear champion or at least clear leadership of the project management innovation journey. This leader may be from senior management (as in Cases 34, 47, 52, and 63), from the management level responsible for project management (e.g., Cases 43, 52, 63, and 75), or from the project team, or from a combination (e.g., Cases 52 and 63). It is also possible that a leader is not explicitly identified (e.g., Case 35); this is most likely to occur when everyone in the organization is expected to align with the initiative in response to a mandatory external trigger such as government regulation. In this case the sponsorship is clearly that of the senior executive but implementation is the responsibility of all, with no exception.

In some cases (e.g., Cases 23, 25, and 43) many employees involved in project work start the innovation as a "low-level" revolution or as an organization-wide initiative. In these cases the project team's innovation actions are designed to develop project management within their organization from the bottom up and directly increase their own capabilities.

Changes in the leadership of the innovation journey may occur in response to the demands of maintaining or developing the innovation specifically in relation to promoting alignment with strategic direction of the organization.

Alignment with Strategic Direction

Of these 10 journeys, we can see wide acceptance of the innovation across the organization in seven cases (23, 25, 35, 43, 52, 63, and 72). Of these seven, two predominant factors resulted in wide acceptance: buying into management direction and development from the ground up. The relationship between sponsorship and the key players (i.e., innovation leadership) appears to be the key connection for enabling alignment of implementation with strategic direction—at least in cases where the senior executive sponsor is aware of the potential relationship.

Case 47 was led by a senior management directive, but some attitudes within the organization and external feedback about this project management innovation were dismissive. This case is particularly interesting, because although there were some dismissive attitudes to the innovation as an improvement in the effectiveness of project management processes, its anticipated benefits relating to the perception of reputation, confidence, and control of the project were accepted.

Cases 25, 43, and 52 all began their innovations with either a strong ground-level involvement, or management leadership that created engagement at many levels. All these innovations were ultimately strongly supported and sponsored by senior management.

Cases 63 and 75 demonstrated both acceptance across the organizations through great visionary leadership in their first journeys, but a failure to integrate staff in sponsorship or top-down decision-making in their second journeys, once the visionary leader was no longer part of the implementation of the innovation.

The presence of strong sponsorship does not in and of itself guarantee a successful innovation. Neither does the presence of strong leadership. The combination of effective integrative leadership supported by sponsorship at the senior management levels of the organization appears from the cases we have analyzed to be the most effective way to create successful project management innovation.

Chapter Summary

In this chapter we compared our 10 detailed cases in terms of the main factors the literature presents as influences on innovation journeys—where and when innovations start, what intervention comes next, what outcomes are anticipated and achieved, who is involved, and what is the impact.

Our cases illustrated clearly that the progression of an innovation journey cannot be understood solely as a sequence of innovation event "labels." The trigger and outcomes for each intervention provide information about the journey to date and where the innovation could go next. Each intervention has an expected outcome, and whether it is achieved or not will influence an organization's decision-making about subsequent interventions.

By comparing and contrasting the cases with each other, we were able to identify that strong organization-level sponsorship combined with effective leadership are most likely to create successful innovation. Effective leaders must be able to win over the culture and attitude of the organization, and must be suitably supported in order to succeed. Clearly the project management champion must be more than an experienced project manager or methodologist; this individual must also be capable of the political entrepreneurship necessary to shape the socialization and learning process of the project managers and others, in order to ensure intergroup safety and integration across the organization.

We now turn from our specific cases toward the bigger picture. In Chapter 8 we consider the major impacts of and on innovation that we have discovered in our analysis of the 10 detailed cases and the original 48 cases, in light of the literature presented in Chapter 2.

Chapter 8

Conceptual Discussion

In this chapter we revisit the most important themes from the literature (as examined in Chapter 2) in light of our empirical findings (as discussed in Chapters 5, 6, and 7). By theorizing our findings in this way, we help to increase understanding in the field of project management as it relates to the process of management innovation, and contribute to theory development in both project management and management innovation.

We begin our conceptual discussion by re-examining the nature of management innovation in light of what we have learned from our example of project management innovation. We then consider how the context of the organization, its history, culture, and power relations impact its ability to innovate, paying particular attention to the role of the external world in triggering management innovation. Once an innovation is underway, the socio-behavioral factors change the path of an innovation's journey. We consider the roles of the key players, such as the executive sponsor, implementation champion, and project personnel, as well as the impact of behavioral dynamics such as creativity, and individual and group dynamics on the innovation process, particularly in reference to adoption, adaption, stabilization, routinization, and diffusion of an innovation. Finally, we discuss the challenges of sustaining innovation. We conclude the chapter by considering the contributions made to the theory. This discussion is focused around management innovation boundaries, continuous improvement, and the dynamics of innovation as a multi-stage process.

Re-examining the Nature of Management Innovation

The theoretical perspectives set forward in Chapter 2 clearly identify four fundamental characteristics of management innovation: intention, newness, change of working practice, and anticipated benefits. These characteristics hold true in many respects for almost all management changes that begin with a business case and are influenced by society's increasing focus on due diligence. This suggests that management innovation is a very common occurrence in today's organizations, and that it deserves much more research and management attention than it has received to date. It is particularly critical to emphasize that management innovation involves—by definition—organizational change, and this has implications in terms of the nature of the strategies that are required to make management innovation successful.

Our research findings show that the most successful management innovations begin with a trigger that is recognized by the executive. Even if the trigger was initially identified by others in the organization rather than by the executive, our data shows that executive power is fundamentally important in initiating change and encouraging an organization to get behind an innovation, and then to persist with refining it to fit. In situations where innovative change is mandated (e.g., Cases 23, 34, 35, and 75), intelligent use of executive power is extremely important in ensuring that the culture and mandate of the management innovation fit the needs of the organization.

An initial innovation is commonly a Radical act (occurring in response to a substantive external trigger) that is followed by a period of Continuous and Convergent innovation, or "polishing." This polishing can be an effective strategy once the organizational fit with the management innovation has been addressed. The innovation is often sustained by a dedicated team that initiates innovation polishing events. They are dedicated to adapting, stabilizing, and routinizing the new management practices within the organization. Initial interventions are focused on, and often yield, the anticipated benefits. If the desired benefits are not realized, subsequent innovation events are implemented to address the gap. Once the organization adopts the new ways of working, polishing actions are valuable; they provide continued strategic and tactical fit to increase value from the innovation. This Continuous/ Convergent innovation activity plays an important role in supporting organizational learning, and contributes to the socialization processes that are important to the individual-identity construction and group safety that are, in turn, necessary to sustain innovation in management practice.

The most successful project management implementation journeys in our study, in terms of those that gained the most value from their project management innovation, are Cases 25 and 35. These two cases both began their innovation journeys by adopting a revolutionary idea (an external project management innovation approach) and then worked to continuously converge ideas and practices, building an innovation that aligned with their organizational needs. The researchers of these cases noted alignment in the project management innovation with regards to a "common frame of reference, knowledge-sharing, high quality, customer satisfaction" (Case 25), and "capability matches customer, subcontractor and supplier expectations" (Case 35). In these cases, the ongoing polishing innovation activity allowed for sustainable innovation, in that innovation was seen as an ongoing process of alignment and fit rather than as a singular event with an end point. These innovation journeys suggest that the value to organizations lies in the journey (the setting of goals, the group dynamics of working toward them, and then responding to the outcomes) as much as the innovation itself. As noted by Eskerod and Riis (2009a) and Thomas and Mullaly (2008), the value of project management improvement activity comes from its ability to bring individuals together to work toward a common goal and to shape a common language, understanding, and identity. Focus during the innovation process must be on "those behavioral and social processes whereby individuals, groups, or organizations seek to achieve desired changes or avoid penalties of inaction" (West, 2002, p. 357), rather than on the innovation.

Some organizations experience initial success when they begin an implementation journey with Continuous-Convergent-type innovations that are based on improving existing practices, and are driven by well-intentioned, lower-level managers. These middle managers spend considerable effort developing an ideal system to meet their own needs (often by introducing externally sanctioned professional standards), which ultimately fails to address the organizational or stakeholders' needs. These management innovations often provide significant benefit to the people actually managing the projects, but these benefits often do not address the higher-level strategic concerns of senior executives. Innovations that begin in this way are often superseded by more Radical and Episodic interventions that are championed by more senior executives, and their decisions about management innovation may not take into account the opinions and/or expertise of the middle-level managers. In our data, we see complex journeys that began with Continuous Convergent interventions being superseded by more Radical Episodic interventions before returning to Continuous Convergent innovation activity—often to the detriment of the original innovation champions, who may leave the organization through this process. We also see a large number of Continuous Convergent innovation activity that never impacts the organization as a whole, and does not result in ongoing sustainable innovation. Likely, this large body of innovation effort addresses non-strategic issues for the organization, and so does not create the ongoing interest and investment necessary to sustain it. This is an example of the scenario described by Green (2008, p. 239), in which a management group mobilizes a specific story line (often the professionalization story) in order to strengthen its position in the organization according to its own political agenda. This activity serves the interests of the internal project management group and the external "guru" industry by increasing the visibility of project management; however, if it does not address strategic issues and solve critical problems of interest to executives, it is not likely to gain the momentum to deliver sustainable innovation.

Although later in this chapter we will consider more specifically the innovation process around project management, in this section we have been concerned with what makes a "management innovation" more than an "emerging practice." Not one of the cases in our database innovated by accident. Each case set forth an intentional action that had been motivated in one of four ways: by the need for satisfaction, power and control, efficiency, or legitimization. These initial motivations clearly reflected the anticipated benefits of implementing a change to working practice. But, in addition to identifying its motivation, for a management change to be innovative one must clearly identify that the change is also new to the job, work team, or organization.

For the data set we investigated, we specifically coded our data for newness; interventions that were not new to the organizations did not become part of our innovation journeys. In other words, the actions of our cases were all, by theoretical definition, management innovations, and were therefore relevant to our discussions.

By definition, innovation must be new, and successful innovation journeys will inevitably become unsustainable after a period of time if they are not designed to adapt to the evolution of the organizational environment and its business strategy on a sustainable and ongoing basis. Successful innovations that begin to decay may themselves become the stimulus for other innovation journeys. As noted by Thompson and McHugh (2002), the rhetoric of innovation demonstrates a particular orientation toward the problems of invention (initial design and development, and in particular newness and novelty) and then implementation and diffusion. However, in practice, "the main priority for management strategy is to create conditions—institutional and cultural—for sustainable innovation through self-generating processes and learning mechanisms in the workplace" (Thompson & McHugh, 2002, p. 253). Here our research findings support the theoretical insights by affirming that successful innovation is an ongoing process without an easily identifiable end point. The ambiguity of the end point of each innovation creates interactive effects between learning, change, and future innovation that drives creativity, socialization, and sustained/routinized action (as per Thompson & McHugh, 2002, p. 254). Innovation develops its own dynamics, tensions, and choices within each specific context/organizational setting, reflecting the genuine differences in management requirements, workforce expertise, and interests. This in turn raises the question of how to classify innovation events and journeys. When does one innovation end and another begin? How do we identify these innovation stages? The work we have done in this study to identify different patterns in innovation journeys (discussed in Chapters 5, 6, and 7) provides a starting point for organizations and researchers to develop an understanding of the nature and status of the innovation journey they are contemplating.

The least valuable innovations we witnessed arose from misidentification of the issues the innovations were intended to address. The organizations misidentified the root causes of the project management symptoms due to a combination of conditions: unrealistic perceptions about what was happening in the organizations; middle managers making decisions about project management without being in a position to evaluate the contextual factors; incapacity of key organizational players to analyze the current position while they were immersed in it; and short-termism stemming from organizational or country culture. Often this misidentification of root causes of the challenges facing organizations results from a "cross-level fallacy" (Green, 2008, p. 237), in which macro and micro levels of analysis are interwoven. In such instances, the subsequent initiation of an innovation that only partly solves a problem is often seen as a series of episodic interventions that aim to fix the situation. Getting the right fix (i.e., solving the problem) makes the innovation effective, but partial or inaccurate innovation leads to further triggers for innovative action. Our data suggests that prior to entering a stage of (Continuous Convergence) polishing, it is important for the organization to take the time to be sure that the correct solution has been implemented rather than develop a partial solution, which is often the case in organizations with a short-term focus.

Impact of Organizational Context, History, and Power Relations

Our exploration of the findings of innovation journeys clearly demonstrates the importance of organizational context, history, and power relations (i.e., the structural/cultural milieu of an organization) in shaping these journeys and enabling innovation. These three factors embedded in the locality in which innovation is happening, at the time it is happening, impact heavily on the three spheres of agency involvement discussed in the literature as critical to shaping innovation: the labor process, employment relationship, and governance.

Organizational Context

In all of our cases, context was one of the key factors influencing the shape of the journey. The contexts represented in the 48 cases included those of communism, post-communism, and capitalism, and developed and developing countries. Different national and economic systems have an influence on governance, labor processes, and employment relations that in turn influence the dynamics of innovation implementation. While we attempted to draw conclusions or themes across these cases by looking for commonalities and differences, the fundamental differences in the contexts from which these cases were drawn cannot be ignored. Although we use words like *learning, socialization,* and *sustainability,* we recognize that these terms are used, understood, and enacted differently by organizations depending on their contexts. For instance, the variations in power relations and national cultures among countries such as China, Canada, and Britain can be used to explain some of the acceptance or resistance to Radical innovation events and the levels of socialization and routinization that were available to support ongoing Consistent-Convergent innovation. In China, the adoption of "best Western practice" is a Radical innovation. But its " Radical" nature is short-lived, as organizations and individuals are more readily able to accept externally imposed innovations and then work to develop ownership and fit over the long term, than are organizations in the more individualistic cultures of Canada, Britain, and Australia. In the latter countries, adoption cannot be taken for granted: processes of socialization and routinizations are required to increase both understanding and uptake of the innovation.

"Micro" political processes can also come into play, as evidenced in the organizations in our study that were involved in internationally supported post-war reconstruction projects or international development projects with powerful funders (such as the World Bank) that required a specific form of project management. In the more individualistic cultures, we saw that imposed changes tended to be resisted, and that Continuous Convergent innovation could easily fade away over time or be overtaken by another competing, more fashionable initiative, rather than leading to ongoing practice improvement.

Professional and Organizational History

Companies in our sample started considering project management at different times and at different points in their own development, and this demonstrated that relevant historical background must also be taken into account when considering innovation implementation. Companies that began their innovation journeys 20 years ago or more were situated in a world where standardization (e.g., project management bodies of knowledge, information technology, supported project management methodology packages, planning and control tools, etc.) was in its infancy, and not globally recognized or understood in the same way everywhere. The project management initiatives of these organizations evolved together with the institutionalization of standards and, in fact, possibly helped shape the professionalization and standardization of the discipline. Organizations that began their journeys in the 2000s did so in a world where project management had been reified through the development of a small number of discrete and competing "best practice" standards and certifications, a market of (and for) these tools, and an entire industry of consultants, trainers, educators, promoters (including professional bodies), and writers who needed to be taken into account. Over time, the institutional context for project management has become more defined, and what are deemed to be "appropriate" project management innovations have become more commoditized. Today organizations seeking to improve their practices are much more likely to adopt a ready-made recipe for project management improvement as mandated by professionals and consulting or "guru" literature than to take the time to clearly identify and address their own specific project management problems. Packaged solutions can be seen as more efficient and more solidly based in best practice than alternative approaches, causing organizations to implement inappropriate solutions to their problems. This in turn can lead to concerns over the faddism of project management as a whole. The increasing definition of standards, and maturity-measurement models associated with these standard implementations, also presents risks in terms of eliminating (1) the interpretive flexibility needed for disparate interests in an organization to "buy into" and support the implementation of the innovation, and (2) the necessary scope for the innovation to evolve to fit the learning and needs of the organization.

In addition to the history of project implementation theory and practice in general, our sample innovation journeys demonstrated that organizational history plays a significant role in the outcome of efforts to innovate around project management practice. For example, in an organization with a history of heroic efforts to deliver profitable projects despite the odds, the implementation of an ISO 9000 certification for project management processes was at first resisted, and then adopted with only a "lip service" approach. In this organization, the combination of historical practice and an ongoing environment in which executives rewarded heroic behavior in individuals meant that the ISO 9000 certification processes only became an issue six weeks before the recertification deadline, when project managers had to update their files to present evidence that they had used the mandated processes. Is it any wonder that project personnel in this organization felt that standardized project management practices simply added overhead and made more work? Is it surprising that turnover in project managers had been almost 90% since ISO 9000 was introduced?

Another, more positive, example of the relationship between organizational history and innovation is Case 52, where the innovation in project management totally changed the management of all aspects of the organization, thereby becoming a major historical event by which all future management innovations were judged. Case 52 illustrates the depth of socialization and routinization evident in successful management innovations.

Power Relations

The success of project management implementation has a lot to do with how people feel about management in general, about the control practices and systems that are in place, about working relationships, and issues related to security and trust. Attitudes toward these factors are determined by the system of governance, employment relations and labor processes in the specific organization. For example, team responsiveness to innovation tasks, the behavior of innovation champions, employee attitudes toward continuous improvement, the resistance to change, the strength of professional identity versus collective values, the locus of power, and intensity of power struggles, are all affected by various contextual factors, such as national or organizational culture. The impact of conflicting power relations, and the consequences of ignoring them and focusing on a purely technical approach to project management implementation, are clearly seen in Case 34, where faculty resistance to a technocratic implementation based on belief in the self-evident value of technical process was more than enough to circumvent the efforts of very highly positioned executive support and expert project champions. Ignoring the power analysis of all key stakeholders likely to be impacted by the innovation is a sure step toward failure. In cases where the innovation is initiated from "bottom up" activities, as in Case 43, power plays less of a role in the early learning and socialization efforts. If, as in this case, management support materializes to support the ground-up initiative, the rollout to the rest of the organization is likely to be successful. However, the absence of powerful support combined with a lack of awareness of power and politics among the champions for bottom-up innovation often leads to failed rollout initiatives. In many of our other cases where hierarchical authority was much less likely to be challenged, external triggers created enough urgency for all organizational members to back the change immediately and then engage in longstanding "improvement" efforts that changed the original implementation substantially—but these organizations always supported the original intent through Constant Convergent innovations designed to increase the fit between the adopted innovation and the needs of the organization. In situations where evidence of failing practice goes unheeded due to a combination of identity, ego, and individualism (e.g., Case 47), external triggers must be significant and sizable to generate action. In such cases, finding a way to integrate the management innovation with identity reconstruction is necessary to ensure that changes are actually embedded in organizational practice and socialized in the work force.

Our cases show that power plays a huge role in the success of innovation. Often the power-savvy executive sponsor (as in Case 25) or innovation entrepreneur (as in Cases 63 and 75) who champions the management innovation plays a significant role in identifying and managing the power influences. This process is critical to shaping the initiative to fit the needs of the organization, and to gaining legitimacy for the innovation. The investment of management support yields value even when an organization is just beginning its journey, and it is often the credibility and power activity of these champions that supports the stabilization of innovative practice.

> There is a lot more focus on [project management] in this company regarding how the project managers can evolve. Project managers have been taken much more serious[ly] and one feel[s] that the company really believe[s] in [project management] and project managers. (PM Management, Case 52.)

Without their facility with power structures within the organization, the innovation often stumbles or fails entirely (as it did in Cases 63 and 75, when the project management champions left the organization). Recognizing management innovation as tied to changes in power structures has implications for the management of such innovations.

The support of the executive for management innovation changes the power structure of the organization. Understanding the potential for management innovation to change power structures requires a Foucauldian approach that moves understanding beyond a focus on the implementation of management innovation as driven by strictly technical/rational knowledge, to incorporate recognition of technical/rational knowledge as an instrument of power (Foucault, 1977, 1985, 2002). Examining how methodically organized action is an effective mechanism through which knowledge (of standards of project management, for instance) affects the social life of an organization, provides fertile ground for exploring how these innovation journeys changed the work lives of individuals. Examining how project management becomes a "regime of truth"—that is, knowledge that has been legitimated and accepted as true by a particular community (Foucault, 1977)—leads us to examine the power relations (productive power, disciplining power, and normalizing power) at work in reinforcing self-discipline through the innovation journey, and in shaping what is known and knowable as organizations move forward in a journey. That is, how does the legitimated knowledge of project management, as it is developed over the course of the innovation journey, influence future innovation activities? Foucault (2002) suggested that there are two mechanisms implicated in regime of truth change. The first is external events, which result in discontinuities that change the problems, risks, and opportunities of actions, and therefore also change the knowledge and actions necessary to address the altered problematization of circumstances. The second is the continuous self-care of individuals in the society or organization. Applying this theory to our cases suggests that Radical interventions are necessary in the case of established truth regimes that no longer fit with the original implementations and that the ongoing polishing and aligning of the more Radical innovations to fit with the organization's needs can be seen as a means of self-care for the individuals involved that shapes actions and knowledge over time. This reflective rationality, exhibited by individuals upon the way that their own actions impact on themselves and others, gives rise to effort that may either sustain or challenge and subvert the truth regime that enacts a particular technical/rational knowledge and practice (project management in this case). This approach suggests a need for further research, including a critical examination of the impact of the "guru" and professional association on the construction of the artifacts and power knowledge surrounding project management innovation, as well as the nature and role of legitimating rhetoric in "selling" project management.

External Pressures and Threats as Triggers

In many cases, innovations in organizations (including management innovations) are initiated not by *internal consensus* but due to external pressures and threats on people/groups/organizations at all levels (organizational climate, support system, market environment, environmental uncertainty, or severity, competition, time pressure, psychological threats to face, or identity). In responding to external pressures of this type, three types of responses are evident in our data. The first is a collective approach to adoption with ongoing improvement and learning to make the innovation fit the needs of the organization (as seen in Cases 23, 35, and 75). The second is adoption in name only, where there is a simulation of investment in new practice but in reality the existing practice is only marginally changed (e.g., Case 47). The third is active resistance, as happened in Case 34. This third response is most likely when the external trigger is more open to interpretation (as in implementations initiated by managers or executives attempting to build their reputation, often influenced by experience imported from another organization), than is, for example, a financial crisis or regulation.

Where it is clear to all constituents that the external trigger requires a response (as in the case of World Bank regulations), and the required response is also clearly delineated (e.g., adopt *PMBOK® Guide* project management practices to meet World Bank regulations), it is much easier to generate the required intergroup collaboration and learning to make the implementation successful. The simulation of investment, particularly around off-the-shelf models, often solves a problem that was not the most likely root of the actual project performance issues—as occurred, for example, with the adoption of ISO 9001 project management in Case 23, and the use of earned value management in Case 47. Where the trigger is less clear, the required action is also usually more contestable. The desire of executives, for example, to implement PRINCE2 because it worked in their previous organization, is a much less solid trigger than is a requirement to address the regulations of the World Bank. In addition, executives who are new to the organization may not have the historical or cultural awareness to plan their implementations to fit within the constraints of organizational culture and demographics.

Key Players

Management innovation is a lengthy process, punctuated with many local interpretations and negotiations of meaning. The duration, ambiguity, and impact of these initiatives mean that many actors play significant roles in the implementation process. "Innovation implementation involves changing the status quo, which implies resistance, conflict, and a requirement for sustained effort [. . .] to overcome these disincentives to innovate" (West, 2002, p. 366). In the words of Buchanan and Badham, "Political behavior [. . .] plays a critical role in translating generic packages into locally workable solutions" (1999, p. 160). In all of our innovation journeys, three key classes of player influenced the dynamics of the implementation. The first was the executive. The second was the project management implementation champion. In many organizations there was a clearly recognizable individual (or more than one) whose efforts influenced how the management innovation was implemented. Finally, several implementation efforts were initiated by project management personnel at various levels within the project management departments of the organization. The involvement of these project personnel in innovation journeys is unique.

Role of Executive

Project management as management innovation is most often triggered by external pressures that are first identified by senior management in their assessment of the organization's performance. The need for innovation usually occurs in projects of enough strategic significance that poor project performance becomes obvious. For example, the construction industry's performance in the global market; large-scale information-technology implementations; public-sector accountability to taxpayers;

external funders of international development and aid projects; increasing customer demands for project performance; and time to market. The senior management perception of failure is grounded in externally imposed beliefs that there is a "right way of managing projects," and that there exists a methodology or external solution to this problem. The combination of the strategically significant project and the external discourse supporting a "best practice" solution triggers executive action (Thomas et al., 2002) to innovate.

In cases where innovation is triggered by external pressures, senior management typically approves the investment and designates appropriate lower levels and/ or external resources to implement. They do not recognize the social, behavioral, and political complexities and managerial and decision-making interdependencies required in change to management practice for which their continuous involvement is necessary. In not seeing the intervention as a management innovation, but rather as a new toolset or procedure for project delivery, they ignore the necessity for them to lead it. In many cases, their interest fades and they move on to investing their scarce time and interests in other challenges, assuming that this issue has been dealt with. Executive focus and support diminishes over time, possibly in line with their perception of urgency.

In some of our cases, executive involvement arose as a mandated action (e.g., Cases 23, 25, and 35). As one key informant in Case 35 stated, "It was only since the adoption of project management methods that the company started to really reform its system [business and cultural attitudes] and establish new management procedures and processes and to run as an economic enterprise." The journey of Case 35 might not work in organizations that do not respond well to mandated actions (for example, those from national cultures with lower respect for authority—as in Case 75, for example).

Role of the Project Management Champion

A lack of senior-level support increases the importance of the role of the champion in the success and sustainability of a project management innovation. In lieu of executive support, where the authority has been delegated to the champion, these individuals can operate as political entrepreneurs (as defined by Buchanan & Badham, 1999) to work the back stage, ownership, and legitimization processes, as well as managing the content of the change. We saw this scenario occur in Cases 63 and 75 in particular. However, where the champion does not have these skills, as was the case for the project managers with Project Management Professional (PMP)® certifications who replaced the original champions in both Cases 63 and 75, we see attempts to routinize that lack the necessary authority, or failures to socialize and legitimize these practices. The original champions had the personal and organizational legitimacy that matched the level of political intensity required to deal with organizational resistance; these qualities were absent in the replacements, whose legitimacy was based on external standards and certification rather than organizational experience and relationships.

In the cases we examined, successful champions took responsibility for improving project performance. They focused not just on project maturity but demanded accountability. They extended their influence beyond the scope of their formal positions, and dealt creatively with constraints to their authority by building coalitions with others at their level or higher. They were distinguished by their tendency to recognize that their lack of formal authority and control, and the resulting power asymmetries, could actually contribute to their ability to build acceptance and socialization into their management innovation. They accomplished this through methods that included teaching and learning. By focusing on performance measurement, and providing meaningful metrics of change and improvement in terms that the senior executives were most likely to accept, they created the perspective that the project implementation was a short-term assignment rather than a career move, even though they were all employees of the organization.

Sometimes, external pressures provide an opportunity for project management executives to enhance their own positions by problematizing the practice of project management as it exists in the organization, and recognizing an externally sanctioned solution. They, in effect, "mobilise these storylines that accord best with their own political agenda" (Green, 2008, p. 239). The executives position the external standards as the solutions and themselves as the saviors, and they put the possibility of other solutions or internally generated learning beyond discussion. Then they convince senior executives that something needs to be done and there is only one solution—theirs—in the expectation that executives will give them the authority to proceed. Green suggested that interpretative flexibility of management fashions, innovations, and improvement benefits serves the interests of both promoters (innovators or consultants) and users (managers to whom they provide persuasive scripts for change) by providing reasonable arguments in support of the desired implementation actions (Green, 2008). Such local implementation of external strategies relies on the contribution, compliance, and cooperation of diverse individuals and groups. Combinations of inexperience, resistance, and inhibition (fear, de-motivation), which are likely to emerge in this process, often severely disrupt implementation, particularly when it comes to diffusing and sustaining innovation.

Role of Project Personnel

In many cases, particularly in the more recent innovation journeys in our sample, project management innovation was initiated by project personnel in response to increasing awareness of professional standards and "best practice" literature. In these cases, the project management innovation tends to be a continuous Convergent effort to bring existing practice into line with project management standards, or to train more people in these standards. Such efforts often explicitly address project management maturity. The results from this type of management innovation can be quite positive in the short term, as adding some rigor and consistency in reporting standards is clearly recognized by senior executives as saving them time (Thomas & Mullaly, 2008). This type of ongoing Continuous Convergent innovation within the project management department can be quite successful, as long as the metrics show improvements over time, and the initiative does not impact other departments too much. There is usually very good buy-in to these initiatives within the project management department, and as new project managers are socialized into the organization's process, these practices become routinized and embedded.

However, as soon as the efforts to improve project management move outside of the project management department, these implementations tend to run into trouble, and are often upset with a Convergent, Episodic or Radical intervention. The project management group usually does not have the political entrepreneurship, legitimacy, or power relations to maneuver a sophisticated organizational change throughout the organization, and the senior management is not likely to be willing or able to devote the time to this initiative unless it can be tied to an urgent external trigger (like the Y2K initiatives of the late 1990s) or a strategic agenda item for one of the executives (such as an enterprise-wide resource planning information system, or a major acquisition or mega-project). In our cases we saw many journeys that had begun as Continuous Convergent internal improvement efforts be disrupted by senior management urgency later in their journeys (see, for example, Case 47 and the first half of Case 75). A great many of our more recent innovation journeys remained in the Continuous Convergent quadrant at the end of our data collection. It remains to be seen if these initiatives will be successfully rolled out to the rest of the organization, or only remain successful within their department.

There were, however, a couple of organizations that began their innovation journeys with Continuous Convergent events, and managed to integrate their practice successfully across the wider organization (see Cases 26 and 74). Here again, however, we cannot be sure that this is the end of the implementation journey, as both of these were initiated relatively recently. It may be that if we were to return to these organizations we would find that their integration journeys had failed (as those in Cases 75 and 63 appear to have done).

Behavioral Dynamics

There are a number of behavioral dynamics involving creativity and mindfulness at the individual and group levels that are impacted by the role of uncertainty that underpins the innovation processes of adoption, adaptation, routinization, and diffusion of innovation. Each of these processes is fundamental to management innovation.

Individual Level Dynamics

For innovation implementation to occur, the context must be demanding, but there must be strong group integration processes and a high level of intra- and inter-group safety and psychological security. Without these group processes in place, individuals can come to fear changes to their roles and see these changes as attacks on their identity. The fear of change and identity uncertainty that are created by significant changes to practice can seriously impact the abilities of individuals to employ the kind of reflexivity that will allow them to realistically assess and tolerate uncomfortable situations, and to learn within those contexts. This in turn hampers the ability of the implementation team to socialize, through learning and identity construction, the project management innovation. The interplay of identities and interests at work at the individual level must be consciously recognized and planned for in project management implementations.

In planning for innovation, it is well recognized that you must assess the organizational capacity for change. However, it must also be recognized that organizational change capacity is not only about the willingness of individuals in the organization to "be motivated" or to "accept ownership," but also involves an extensive and complex interplay of identities and interests (Boddy & Buchanan, 1992; Buchanan & Badham, 1999). Care must be taken to recognize the role of "identity construction" in the adoption of specific professionally certified project management implementations. For instance, an innovation that moves an organization from a *PMBOK® Guide* to a PRINCE2 project management methodology (or vice versa) does not simply involve a change in methods; for many project managers who are PMP® certification holders, such an innovation could be interpreted as a direct attack on their identity and competence. The same effect could occur where methodologies like the *PMBOK® Guide* and PRINCE2 are introduced into an organization in which project managers have previously been free to employ whatever tools worked for them. Failure to recognize the human dynamics of identity and interests that are intertwined with what people do and how they do it is sure to result in resistance. In cases where the innovation champion's identity is conflated with professional membership or ideas of expertise, management innovation may be seen as self-evident, and efforts to justify or rationalize the change may be ignored or underplayed (see, for example, Case 34, where a PRINCE2-certified project manager and an executive lead the PRINCE2 implementation).

Organizations with long-term employee relations have stronger organizational memories than those of newer organizations, and project managers are likely to run into more resistance to change in project practice unless care is taken to involve project personnel not only in the implementation of the changes, but also in their design and development. Recognizing the importance of involving longer-term employees will reduce the likelihood of the project management innovation leading to severe turnover, lack of loyalty, or disruption to labor processes, or having a negative impact on employee relations. In addition, these repositories of organizational memory can also provide the contextual and historical information that project management implementation personnel will need to understand the problems that the innovation is meant to address, and help to customize the implementation to more effectively address these problems. On the other hand, these long-term organizational members can also be a source of resistance to change, as they may feel the need to protect existing practices that are tied into their social identity construction and employment relations with the organization. If organizations have experienced difficulty in innovating management practice in the past, this history can lead to organizations avoiding future efforts to implement change.

Group Dynamics

Project management implementation, like any management innovation, is a group activity. It entails social, behavioral and political processes. In order to be successful, an innovation implementation must be an integrated effort. According to West (2002), one of the most important aspects of this is inter-group safety, which means addressing the conflicting interests and subcultures within and between groups. Contributors to a sense of safety include psychological security, trust, and consistency in the senior manager's behavior. In Case 63, the project management implementation champion's efforts to develop a system of simple training to be administered to all employees is an example of an effort to diminish intergroup concerns and jealousies.

Clarification and insurance of commitment to group objectives is achieved through participation in decision-making and developing group members' integration skills. This is evident in Case 23's need to create an organizational unit as the focus of project management improvement to capture the buy-in of the project managers who facilitated commitment, and in Case 25's investment in communities of practice and ongoing socialization efforts. Adoption of practices in both cases was facilitated by their national cultures (Chinese in Case 23 and Danish in Case 25) and commitment to organizational outcomes, but further action relating to group integration and commitment was required to focus attention on the role of project management as distinct from other initiatives.

Senior management behavior that supports project management in real time is important, but equally important is past executive behavior. As evidenced in the university example (Case 34), once the faculty were able to reject the initial project management implementation efforts, future Episodic efforts to reinforce the chosen methodology continued to fail for the same reason that the initial implementation failed—the management had not attended to the socio-political and behavioral aspects of the process of implementation. With each further "fix" journey the organization engaged in without dealing with these challenges, the more the response of senior executives to back down in the face of opposition was reinforced, leading to greater future resistance. The senior management's historical behavior influences what is possible today, and what happens today in turn sets the scene for how the group will act for future interventions.

Creativity

Creativity is a necessity precursor for invention, but it also plays a fundamental role in enabling organizations to implement workable management innovations that are shaped to their particular needs and contexts. Creativity is subjective, context-specific (i.e., defined by the level of structural flexibility, freedom, time, and participation in decision-making) and judged on outcomes (see West, 2002). This means that the creative outcome of both individuals and groups are necessary for a complete innovation process. Several of our most successful examples involved ongoing creative, participative processes used to develop commitment to an internal solution that was perceived to be better than externally advocated project management solutions. In these cases the power of commitment to, and ownership of, internally and creatively developed models of project management generated significant tangible and intangible benefits that would not have been attributed to an externally sourced solution.

According to Thompson and McHugh (2002, p. 256), "experiencing innovation without creative involvement is likely to be simply 'the exchange of one obligation for another.' " In such cases, intrinsic motivation and discretion are of the essence (Thompson & McHugh, 2002), and tend to emerge and evolve from perceived levels of ownership of the innovation process as a whole, and on outcomes perceived as mutually beneficial. The positioning of innovation as deeply connected to anticipated benefits may potentially compensate for the lack of creative involvement of affected organizational members and stakeholders. In a number of the cases we studied, there was little evidence that there was adequate space and time for creativity to play a significant role in initial innovation events; critical external triggers motivated buy-in to innovation efforts more quickly than the creative processes envisioned in the literature. In these cases, crises seemed to play a role in motivating behavior that would otherwise be generated through participation in a creative process.

Organizations that find themselves involved in Episodic interventions and in particular "fixes" or "serial fixes" are far removed from creativity, and appear to be simply seeking quick solutions to problems that in fact require a more creative innovation. To avoid this trap, they need to be clear on the goals of a management innovation and the advantages of an external solution before taking this route of fixing. Failure to realistically evaluate the problem and match it to a suitable fix will likely lose the individual creativity and ownership that results from mindfully engaging in the co-creation process of innovation.

Mindfulness

Our cases suggest that mindfulness in implementing management innovation (Weick & Sutcliffe, 2001)—rather than the mindless adoption of a managerial fad (Abrahamson, 1991)—is critical for increasing an organization's understanding of fit and alignment, and the role these factors play in generating valuable innovation journeys. "Mindfulness" is here examined at the organizational level, and concerns the ongoing adaptation of management expectations in the context of the unexpected, based on the awareness of multiple perspectives and contexts. Innovation, understood as an explicit venture into the unexpected, is dependent on organizational mindfulness (Swanson & Ramiller, 2004) for success. Organizationally mindful decisions are associated with discriminating choices of alternatives that best fit the unique circumstances of the firm, rather than being based on the familiar or imitating what other firms are doing (Fiol & O'Connor, 2003). The need for mindful innovation produces a requirement for practitioners to be critical consumers of information, examining innovation ideas for their local validity without being afraid to shape and polish these interventions to fit better with their own organizations. Examining exactly where and how our case organizations attained and retained this critical level of mindful innovation is important to helping other organizations achieve their goals.

In some cases (e.g., 23, 25, 35, and 72), sustained routinization was not an issue or goal of the innovation implementation process, but occurred as a natural result of the companies' efforts to fit the project management implementation to their organization. Because these organizations were mindful of their own particular contexts and engaged in sustained routinization, a positive but initially unplanned outcome was achieved. This was particularly evident in our cases from China (23, 35, and 72), but was also visible in Case 25 from Denmark and Case 75—first journey—from Canada. In these journeys, project management implementation was not about checking boxes, but about arriving at and maintaining processes that worked in their contexts, and were flexible enough to accommodate emergent requirements.

In our Chinese cases, we saw a difference in the adoption of project management between companies with construction/engineering projects versus those with primarily IT projects. The construction-oriented companies needed to institute project management innovations in the early 1990s as a precondition for obtaining loans for infrastructure projects from the World Bank. This externally mandated change to practice was accepted at the highest levels in the organizations, and project management practices were whole-heartedly adopted without significant initial change. Over time, these practices were adapted to work within the Chinese context and culture through a process of continuous improvement geared toward collective company and project success.

In the IT world, there was no externally mandated requirement for project management. However, projects were not as successful as customers would have liked and so there was significant pressure to improve the delivery of projects. IT best practices embedded in ISO 9000 and CMM methodologies came to be recognized in the mid-2000s, and in our Chinese cases (23, 35, and 75), organizations attempted to improve project management by adopting them. Adoption of these practices, which were related to organizational learning processes, helped the organizations identify key project management practices that needed further refinement (specifically, status reporting). These processes were then elaborated, based on internal experience and external review of "best practice" guidance. In these cases, there was no evidence of resistance to these new approaches. This can be explained by the Chinese culture's focus on action toward collective success. In this context, culture appeared to be the key integrating mechanism that allowed for rapid socialization, adoption and routinization of the innovation.

Another example of mindful innovation arose from a comparison of two high-value innovation journeys (China, 35, and U.S., 55) in which the latest recorded innovation event was to prune large project management infrastructures (developed over a long period of time) back to manageable and organization-wide principles that could be applied to all projects all of the time. The critical reflection and mindfulness necessary to revisit successful and well-accepted practice and to simplify is critical to ensuring on an ongoing basis that the innovation fits with corporate needs, and in sustaining the innovation efforts. The mindful desire to innovate for the purpose of gaining competitive advantage allowed these firms to continue to improve on practice, even though they had already attained success and ongoing acceptance.

Role of Uncertainty

It is apparently paradoxical but true that uncertainty may be as important to innovation as sustained momentum and routinization. Systematized innovation processes can hamper creativity. If you get too comfortable with the routinized processes, innovation stops because you lose sensitivity to, and the ability to adapt to, new and emergent circumstances. In this way, perceived success in dealing with external threats or internal job design might remove the very spark needed for creative endeavor. In these circumstances uncertainty encourages creative innovation, not invention, because the sense of threat motivates people to accept the socialization required for adoption and routinization of new ideas.

The importance of uncertainty to successful innovation is clearly illustrated by two of our innovation journeys (Cases 47 and 55), both of which took place in organizations involved in the defense industry. Both organizations had invested in their project management practice for long periods of time and both believed in and had a reputation for practicing "world-class" project management. Case 47 was subjected to serious external pressure from its customers, who were becoming more sophisticated about project management, and recognized the lack of project results. The internal project management groups of Case 55 developed extensive project management methodologies (extending over nine shelf-feet of binders) through continuous improvement efforts. In their latest innovation (a fix), three individuals over two years worked with the internal groups to prune the methodology, because project managers were chafing at the magnitude of the project management methods and techniques demanded of them, and clients were questioning the need for all of the overhead.

The journey diagrams of these two journeys look the same. However, the outcomes are substantially different, largely because of these two organizations' differing responses to uncertainty. Case 47 substantially rejected the evidence that should have generated uncertainty in its project management practices, and refused to engage in mindful critique and innovation. This organization invested in innovation events that paid little attention to socialization, learning, or routinization of new management practice, but resulted in large gains in legitimacy. The organization realized significant short-term financial impact from these innovation events, which researchers did not expect would to generate value in the long term because practice, individual attitudes, and project results had not changed. In Case 55, the long-term value trend was positive, and the satisfaction and use of the new methods was demonstrated in the behavior, attitudes, and project results. These two organizations, working in very similar contextual situations and responding to similar client-driven concerns, engaged in significant management innovation activity. However, one organization rejected any need to recognize uncertainty and engaged in activity that supported its existing identity construction around "best practice" project management, while the other embraced the uncertainty about its practice and accepted the challenge to mindfully examine and refine existing "best practice." The resulting practice in these two organizations reflects very different value trends, levels of acceptance and routinization, and outcomes. Our observations about internal group dynamics, intra-team socialization and integration, pruning, revising, and sustaining efforts confirm West's suggestion of the necessity of these inputs into longer-term success of management innovation (2002).

Once the implementation is successful, the uncertainty about the quality of the project management practice is eliminated or reduced, and executive interest wanders. The impetus for continued innovation, learning, and routinization is similarly reduced, and once-successful innovations can fall into disrepair.

For example, consider again Case 75: once the external perceived threat of poor project management practices was rectified and recognized as having been addressed—when the organization won PMI awards, and so forth—uncertainty about whether the organization knew how to manage projects was resolved, innovation ceased, and over time, with turnover, the internalized understanding of how to manage projects evaporated. Until renewed senior management concerns about lack of project performance introduced new levels of uncertainty that were resolved through quick investment in "best practice" PMO practices rather than reasserting the original innovation's socialized behaviors (i.e., re-establishing how to do project management here). Our study showed that the moment uncertainty is perceived as having been dealt with, learning stops, as identity and confidence associated with knowing how to do projects ("we are okay") and routinization become firmly established. This is counter-intuitive to sustained innovation, which requires a position of humility and continuous questioning of the status quo that is not comfortable to many individuals.

In times of uncertainty, institutional activity designed to recognize "best practice" is often adopted to artificially increase comfort levels within organizations in regard to project management practice without the need to invest the energy into actually figuring out why current practices do not work. The recent conservatism evident in the most recent innovators, specifically in cases that have only a single innovation event, also provides evidence of the influence of professional associations and standardizations in reducing organizational uncertainty with respect to innovation actions or outcomes. It is asserted that uncertainty can be reduced by adopting a solution that appears to have been tested. This approach acts to minimize the organization's uncertainty about the usefulness of the innovation, but it also leads to a reduced likelihood of the organization's questioning or modifying the solution to fit its own needs.

Sustaining Innovation

Our cases support the theoretical view that sustaining innovation is problematic. The influence of power and political savvy has been seen to strongly influence both what is innovated and also how it is adopted, and consequently maintained and sustained, in an organization. Senior management sponsorship, using a variety of "persuasive" strategies and behaviors if necessary, will influence the sustained attitude to the innovation—for example, in Case 25, executive support and actions of a bottom-up innovation provided ongoing innovation; less subtly in Cases 23, 35, and 72, senior management desire was accepted without question. In Case 34, however, the strongly persuasive powers of the senior management were still not sufficient for at least part of the workforce. The innovation continued to be rejected, even though it was ultimately used to restructure the organization. The senior management of Case 34 realized only part of the anticipated benefit and continued to apply fixes in the hopes of achieving further benefits, without ever addressing the underlying cause of the resistance. In Cases 23, 35, and 72, even following the senior executive lead, it was the local adaptation that made the project management implementation take root and be successful, demonstrating West's (2002) ideas about the role of contribution, compliance, and cooperation in innovation success.

Incoming innovation leaders "wishing to make their own mark on events" (Buchanan & Badham, 1999, p. 164) may struggle (e.g., in Case 34) with gaining suitable socialization and routinization that is required to sustain an innovation past the first flush of compliance promoted by senior management. Even with political skills, without the socialization required, the innovation will not sustain past the loss of the champion (e.g., Cases 63 and 75).

Innovations that rely on external validation and authorities for legitimacy often do not have the gravitas to withstand local adaptation or resistance caused by uncertainty and lack of trust in the methods. When interest and championship at senior levels wane, then if the innovation has not been routinized and socialized, there is no buy-in and the innovation has not become embedded in daily practice and the innovation will also fade away.

Fitting an existing solution in the form of standards to a sometimes strategically created problem (a situation described as the "garbage can" approach to strategic decision-making by Cohen, March, & Simon, 1972) can lead to difficulties with implementation, as the standard solution may not have the interpretive flexibility necessary to support the innovation. The lack of flexibility in the preferred standard solutions creates a strong potential for resistance. The only card such solutions offer is that of the legitimacy of external standards. Sustaining project management as an innovation most frequently becomes a problem when there is resistance or managerial abandonment, or the innovation fades out or loses out to another "innovation." When senior management turns its attention onto the next big thing (external) or the next crisis (internal), all the sustained good practices can be lost.

The project management industry has made efforts to create institutionally recognized innovations to provide unquestionable and self-evident support to project management champions at lower levels in organizations. These standard innovations help low-level champions in their efforts to gain authority to overcome vested interests of other groups within the organization. Standardizing approaches like this, however, totally ignores what we know about the group processes of adaptation and local revision that are so important to supporting and sustaining both creativity and buy-in for the project management innovation. Project management implementations that focus too heavily on audit and control, and efforts to ensure that standardized practices are followed, tend to drive the creativity out of project management by focusing on rule-following and box-checking. Project management maturity implementation efforts with a focus on standardization have a particular tendency to fall into this trap. This was clearly evident in Case 23's original attempts at innovation through adoption of ISO 9000 project management standards (although this organization realized the problem and moved on to more creative innovations). This pattern of declining sustainability once the project management emphasis focused on standardization and control was also evident in the second half of Case 75's innovation journey, where the organization started to implement standardized project management offices and portfolio management rather than reinforcing the formerly successful project management implementation.

Contributions of this Research

We now turn our attention from the contributions the management innovation literature makes to our understanding of project management innovation to the contributions our examination of one particular type of management innovation (project management implementation) across organizations and across time can make to the larger innovation debates.

Management Innovation Boundaries

In Chapter 2 we highlighted the serious gap in research on the implementation of management innovation. This is a well-recognized area of neglect in the literature to date, and as we outlined in Chapter 2, the challenges are many. However, this study highlights another challenge that was not documented in the literature we reviewed; namely, the boundaries of what constitutes a management innovation are not well defined, either in practice or in research.

It is very difficult to assess when an organization began an innovation journey and even more difficult to determine when the journey ended. A substantial number of organizations in our sample reported only a single innovation event. However, it is impossible to determine from the data whether these were the first and only innovation events for any given organization, or whether the innovation event was the beginning of a much more substantial journey. That is, the latest innovation event recorded in our data collection process was not necessarily the final event in the organization's journey in relation to that innovation. From updating three of our cases, we obtained evidence that the last innovation events collected in 2008 for these organizations were far from the last steps in their journeys. There was also evidence in many other cases that study participants were planning for future innovation events.

Research is a time-bounded activity and it must by nature identify a start and end, if only in the interests of data collection. In this study, data was collected between 2006 and 2008, but we also asked our participants to remember back to the earliest point at which project management was brought into the organization. While we recognize the problems of memory, our data was crosschecked by document review and interviews with many people in each organization, so we feel fairly confident that we have identified the first intervention. We cannot say, however, with any kind of equivalent certainty, that the last innovation event we recorded was the end of the innovation journey for any given organization. In fact, we are more certain that it was in fact *not* the end of the innovation journey for most of these organizations, especially given that theorists such as West have suggested that it is the sustainability of the innovation that determines the success of innovation journeys.

Survey research exploring management innovation aims for large sample size and typically looks at management innovations within a set time period of the survey for all types of innovations in an organization at one time. The challenge here is that the stage of the innovation journey is not taken into account in this type of analysis. Is the event a beginning, an ending, or a sustaining event? How can scholars compare these different management innovations in any meaningful way if they are at different stages in the innovation journey?

Case study research that relates to innovation encounters similar problems, in that the question of how to include the history of the innovation, analyze the observed innovation, and then determine at which stage of the innovation journey the company is located would be a difficult assessment, if it were ever undertaken. Given that most case studies look at single innovation events taken out of the context of the journey, some comparison of apples and oranges certainly occurs in attempts to learn across these cases.

Continuous Improvement

The literature suggests that management innovation should lead to continuous improvement, because innovation is about measurable outcomes leading to a better state. However, we note that "continuous improvement" appears to be understood differently in different contexts, and these context variations can influence the outcomes of apparently similar innovation journeys. In our figures, Continuous improvement journeys are represented in the Persistent quadrant as multiple persistent events (these look like flowers). Qualitatively, these journeys can be differentiated. For example, in the Chinese cases, continuous improvement results in new project management practices that are quite different from those in place at the starting point. Our data provides several examples where an organization adopted an externally imposed project management methodology in order to meet external demands, and then proceeded to continuously improve the project management practices in response to specific unique internal demands. The resulting practice, developed over a substantial period of time, had some semblance to the beginning point but was significantly different from it, in that practices were made to fit with the context and culture of the organization, and the organizational and project environments.

Almost all other examples of this journey, arising in other national contexts, reflect innovation events that focus on refining compliance to the core model; these compliance-oriented innovations were adopted because in contexts where turnover, diversity, and individualism is high, continuity rests more heavily in the standards than in the organizational membership or national culture. Where continuous improvement means simply building additional templates (standardization, routinization, recipe-writing, and recipe-following) onto existing systems, it risks becoming obsolete and unreflective of the real needs of the organization and its practitioners. Evidence of the demise of PMOs when this happens is widespread (Hobbs et al., 2008, and Case 63). In order for innovation to thrive through Continuous Convergent interventions, a clear link to learning and assessment must accompany an emphasis on standardization, socialization, and routinization. Implementation journeys in our data set in which the questioning and learning aspects were lost were soon replaced with more Radical interventions.

Repeated Convergent Episodic interventions, or "fixes," also need to be carefully examined to determine—from the context—whether they are effective innovations or if they are simply habitual or safe investments that deflect attention from the project management practices for a period of time. If they are used to avoid doing the heavy work, including the kind of critical and mindful examination of practice that is necessary to develop a thorough understanding of what needs to be done, these episodic interventions are not likely to provide long-term solutions.

Dynamics of Management Innovation Implementation

Adapting the operationalization by Street and Gallope (2009) of the pace and scope of organizational change to examine innovation events provides a foundation for further study of the dynamics of management innovation. It supports our analysis of the dynamics of management innovation across time for individual cases by allowing us to look at change in the nature of innovation events and the implications of changes in event types. The innovation journey segments we identified and named were based on the theoretical description of pace and scope, the generic types of innovation, and the journey—that is, what it would mean to move from a persistent innovation event to a tectonic and back again or from a punctuated to a series of persistent innovation events. Investigating the journey in this way allows deeper insight into the interwoven nature of the triggers, actors, and outcomes involved in longer innovations. It allows question such as, "What does this sequence of interventions mean?" and "Is it a good fit or a naïve attempt to minimize uncertainty?"

Journey-mapping presents a high-level view of which innovations are implemented. As with any practice-based investigation, the context for each organization reveals the whole story. Returning to a situation discussed earlier, at first glance the journeys of Cases 47 and 55 are identical, but in context they have quite different innovation experiences. Case 47 presented itself as successful, even though in a complicit external presentation of the implementation (Maylor & Brady, 2010) it was apparent that what the journey map captured was the organization acting as if it were successful. In Case 55, internal project management groups developed extensive project management methodologies through continuous improvement efforts. In its last innovation (a fix), three individuals over two years worked with internal groups to prune the methodology, because project managers were chafing at the magnitude of the project management methods and techniques demanded of them. One case resulted in significant change in practice, while the other simply paid lip service to any need for change. This example highlights the need for any research into management innovation to be founded on rich contextual information, as well as the study of innovation events, in order to make sense of the socio-political and behavioral dynamics of the innovation process.

The fact that our mapping was tested against our 48 cases provides some face validity for its claim to helping us understand the dynamics of management innovation. The common stories and high-level journeys of our cases, coupled with the organizational context, provide insight into the effects and possible future direction for organizations contemplating innovation journeys. From a practical perspective, this mapping tool provides real value to organizations and consultants in evaluating where an organization is located in terms of its innovation journey, and what kinds of future innovation events are likely to be most effective.

Methods of Study

The methods developed for this study of identifying all innovation events, journey segments, and entire innovation journeys, and then characterizing them with contextual, trigger, intent, intervention, and outcome data, presents a more comprehensive approach to the study of management innovation than has previously been available. This contribution alone increases the capacity to compare cases in this literature more meaningfully. It also provides a means for unraveling the process of innovation to explore the impact of mindfulness, uncertainty, and the individual and group behaviors of innovation—ideas that have been discussed since the 1990s but rarely empirically examined in as much detail.

Another of the contributions of our work to methodology is the longitudinal cross-case study of the implementation of management innovation. By examining the implementation of a similar management innovation across organizations and exploring the contextual variables that differ for each case, we provide insight into the dynamics of management innovation implementation that is not possible to those who are looking at different innovations. In effect, our examination of similar innovations holds constant some of the contextual variables that would otherwise influence the innovation and interpretation. For instance, all of these implementation journeys could be expected to be at least aware of, if not influenced by, the globalization of project management professional institutions and the project management training industry in the last decade. Thus they share some common input to "best practices."

Project Management as Management Innovation

Given the extant and long-standing definition of "innovation" as "the implementation of ideas new to the locality," and of "management innovation" as "changes to processes, practices and structures with an intent to improve performance," there is no question that project management implementation can effectively be analyzed as a form of management innovation. This approach facilitates the examination of project management implementation as more than the adoption of a toolset, methodology, or system at lower levels of operation in the organization, but as a strategic organizational change important to the organization's capacity for strategic delivery and performance.

Our first analysis of the data resulted in Figure 8.1, which attempted to encapsulate a generalized vision of the process.

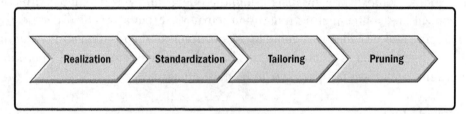

Figure 8.1. Process of project management innovation

Initial examination of all 65 cases raised an interesting commonality in what was implemented by organizations at similar levels of project management maturity. Figure 8.1 illustrates this process by reflecting the stages that an innovator typically goes through in progressing innovation. Most successful journeys begin with executive-level urgency, triggered by external events or conditions, or by executive agendas, and end with continuous improvement within the project department (see Cases 23, 35, 72, and 75 [early journey]).

The initiation of innovation stems from a realization that there is a need for action. This is followed by the initiation of action by selecting and adopting a project management practice. This first realization and subsequent intervention is most likely externally triggered and may or may not be aligned with the business needs of the organization (depending on the level of sponsorship of the management innovation, awareness of options, capability of current employees and management, etc.). Many initial adoptions involve standardized solutions or "best practices" and are implemented to replicate what is understood to be good practice—what have been effective for other organizations. These changes bring in new ways of working that are anticipated to be of benefit to the employees and the organization—or, ideally, both.

As organizations increase their level of practice maturity in relation to the project management they have chosen, they cycle through a process in which they increase the efficiency of practice through standardization and routinization, and then increase effectiveness by adapting the implementation to meet the driving organizational needs. This tailoring stage of innovation can be followed by efforts to further increase the efficiency of the tailored implementation by pruning away any extraneous practices. This process of balancing efficiency concerns with concerns of effectiveness gives rise to situations in which people invested in polishing a particular type of implementation can find themselves shaken to the core when shifts in organizational needs demand project management practice be integrated across the organization, renovated, or revolutionized. In some cases, organizations become stuck in one of these phases, continuously polishing their practices but failing to generate the organizational-level support or interest needed to implement the required diffusion of practice, renovation, or revolutionary change that would move them to the next stage of project management development.

Examining project management in this way necessitates a much more sophisticated assessment of the triggers, intents, actions, and outcomes of such efforts. Interventions such as these, in complex adaptive systems, must be carefully monitored and supported by executives and project personnel alike. The socio-political and behavioral implications of such interventions need to be carefully assessed and managed if project management is to successfully support organizational needs. Failure to pay attention to these aspects of project management implementation, as occurred in Cases 34 and 47, can damage the reputation of project management in those organizations, and possibly contribute to its being seen as a "fad" without real organizational value.

Finding the correct fit between the selected management innovation event and the organization's culture has been shown to be an important step toward delivering management value from investment in improving project management practice (Thomas & Mullaly, 2008, pp. 287–333). Implementing management innovation events that are more easily adapted to, and can be more easily socialized into, the existing culture of the organization means that the changes are more easily stabilized, routinized, and normalized, and ultimately become embedded within the practice of the organization. It is also important to recognize that the most appropriate type of innovation event changes over time, even for a single organization, as contextual factors change. As the innovation journey progresses, the value organizations seek also changes. The innovation journey involves a dynamic and continuous process of picking the right process (initiation and adoption), to aligning the right model (adaption), to stabilizing.

Interpreting Figure 8.1 in relation to the management innovation literature provides further insights into the cyclical nature of the management innovation journey, and its stages of initiation, adoption, standardization, routinization, and adaptation. The initiation of management innovation entails realizing that change is necessary. The second step in the implementation of project management, which we labeled "standardization," involves the innovation processes of adoption, standardization, and routinization. Our final two steps, "tailoring" and "pruning," relate specifically to the processes of adaptation and the application of creativity, mindfulness, and co-creation to fit the management innovation to the organizational needs. However, in looking at the cases in greater detail, we see that this is not a linear process, but one that can be cycled through, returning to previous parts of the process a number of times, depending on the starting point, outcomes of innovation interventions made in previous stages of the process, and external and internal context.

Some might ask at this point why organizations need to go through all this process: why can't they simply adopt the "best practice" models endorsed by professional associations, consultants, or other organizations? Our answer is twofold. First, this is exactly what we saw most organizations doing. This diagram suggests that once a need is recognized, the first step for most organizations is to adopt best practice models from external sources. The next step, however, is almost always to adapt them to address the unique needs of each organization through a process of trial and error and learning. Second, the innovation literature tells us that this trial and error, learning by doing, creative adaptation, and reflection is a necessary and in fact mandatory requirement to successfully embed the management innovation in the fabric of everyday practice. Sustainable innovation requires ongoing, mindful critique of existing practice combined with significant attention to engaging the creativity and ownership of employees to increase the stabilization and routinization of the new practices. The tailoring and pruning efforts increase the organization's understanding and ownership of the new practices while ensuring that the practices continue to meet the needs of the changing context and organization. The journey is not something to be optimized but rather the journey is what enables the management innovation to successfully moderate the relationship between practice and the changing organizational and environmental context.

Finally, previous investment in project management can be destroyed by more recent innovation events that change project management practice without building on and reinforcing expertise. In Cases 47 and 75, where an innovation event triggered a negative value trend for the project management innovation, the triggering event was driven by a move back toward a standardized approach to control-oriented project management that had little to do with the challenges the organization faced in its previous project management implementation.

Our findings also support the arguments as set out in Chapter 2 with respect to the importance of interpretive flexibility, and differences between external solutions and the new management practices that are eventually embedded within the organization. The evidence provided here suggests that the most successful project management innovations are those that include a liberal dose of creativity and tailoring of the solution to the context and needs of the organization, which supports the notion that the reality of project management implementations is normally much different than the advice set out in existing literature and guidelines. This is especially true in cases where research and literature advocate a more strategic role for project management: the evidence suggests that most project management implementation efforts today still address the technical and operational aspects of project management (writ small), rather than the strategic decision-making roles embedded in such areas as portfolio and program management. This does not necessarily imply that the advice is wrong: it could be that current management innovation around project management practice is not meeting the needs identified by researchers. Either way, this situation does suggest that the need for interpretive flexibility that garners support for innovation being realized even in situations where maturity models and strict guidelines and audits of practice are thought to hold sway.

Summary

Through a broader lens, this chapter builds a coherent view of innovation, relating the conceptual perspectives from literature as set out in Chapter 2 to the empirical perspectives of Chapters 5, 6, and 7.

Innovation is truly impacted by many significant factors. Some exist around an organization before, during, and after innovation—such as organizational context and history, as well as power relations, including cultural, structural, and political dimensions. Others, such as external pressure and threats, act as triggers for innovation that closely affect the who, what, and how of involvement required in organizational changes, and the role uncertainty plays in initiating change. The ongoing dynamics of innovation includes an active interplay between those involved in innovative organizational changes—the key players, sponsors, executive, champion, project personnel, and the individual. This discussion touches on the dynamics around creativity, adoption, and sustainability of innovations.

We concluded this chapter with a view on how this research contributes to our understanding of management innovation, both in our research method and in our findings. Examining the interleaved components of an innovation throughout its journey and across organizations implementing a similar management innovation allows us to explore the impact of mindfulness, uncertainty, and the individual and group behaviors of innovation and insights into the dynamics of management innovation. We confirmed project management as a good example of management innovation. We propose a theory of how and why organizations evolve their way to effective project management practice rather than simply adopt a set of tools and techniques by observing organizations who, after initial realization of what innovation is required, increase their level of practice maturity by cycling through a process in which they increase the efficiency of practice through standardization and routinization, then increase effectiveness by adapting the implementation to meet the driving organizational needs through innovation events associated with tailoring and pruning. This model incorporates learning from management innovation and we believe can be generalized out to explain other kinds of management innovations besides project management.

We turn now to Chapter 9 to bring together the lessons and teaching from this work in conclusions, possibilities for future research, and guidance for practice.

Chapter 9

Conclusions and Possibilities

We set out in this research to present lessons learned from examining the project management implementation journeys undertaken by 48 organizations over a period of up to 30 years. By identifying the types of interventions used across time and at specific times (e.g., first and latest interventions), we have identified patterns that provide evidence about the actuality of how project management is implemented and innovated in organizations today. Our study contributes knowledge to what were previously significant gaps in the fields of management innovation and project management. By closely observing the differences in experience across organizations when implementing this one particular organizational innovation, we were able to contribute empirical evidence to the study of project management implementation, as well as to the field of management innovation more broadly, by integrating social and behavioral considerations with organizational and environmental contextual factors. We operationalized our analysis by adopting an organizational change framework— adapting, and eventually modifying and enhancing it to make it more useful for our analysis of management innovation journeys.

This monograph provides an empirical exploration of historically reconstructed project management implementation journeys, paying particular attention to innovation events recognized and reported by a cross-section of informants, and documented in organizational files. Drawing from management literature on innovation and organizational change, we contextualized innovation events in terms of pace and scope to identify four types of innovation actions: Persistent (Continuous Convergent), Tectonic (Episodic Convergent), Punctuated (Episodic Radical), and Turbulent (Continuous Radical). Examining the occurrence of these events in the empirical data made evident four prominent simple innovation journeys. The complex innovation journeys of specific organizations combine these simple innovation journeys as they work to integrate, fix, revolutionize, or polish project management innovations.

Consideration of the innovation journeys of the more active innovators in our data demonstrated in practice the complex multiple use of the various types of innovation events. Cross-case comparisons of multi-stage journeys of these organizations with the early stages and simple innovation journeys of other organizations that were just starting out on their project management journeys were informative. Comparisons provided a starting point from which to study innovation events empirically, and facilitated the theorizing of management innovation processes. This in turn allowed us to provide practical recommendations for organizations that are contemplating the process to improve project management.

Organizations that generate value from their project management implementation not only go through the process of innovating, but also actually seek alignment of the full implementation with their organizational and business strategy. In this way they assure that project management supports their business needs. Consequently, when their business needs change, project management also needs to change in response. Ideally, stages of the innovation process are revisited, often from differing starting points, depending on the nature of the strategic change. The manifold nature of both the innovation events and the innovation journeys supports recent applications in the literature of complexity theory in management that calls for recognition of organizations and projects as complex adaptive systems.

The analysis presented in this monograph and the propositions emanating from our research complement in many important ways three other monographs: Williams (2007) on learning in project environments; Thomas and Mullaly (2008) on the value of project management; and Cicmil, Crawford, Cooke Davis & Richardson (2009) on the complexity of projects.

Key Insights

Much as executive-level support is a critical success factor for projects, our data clearly demonstrates that this kind of support must also be in place for successful project management implementation. Successful innovation journeys were supported by strong executive interest combined with a clear, externally driven trigger, addressed a strategically important organizational issue, and exhibited strong project management championship. Most often this resulted in Episodic (often Radical/Episodic) innovations. Most journeys that began without strong executive support or effective project management championship resulted in continuous improvement efforts that never influenced wider organizational management or provided significant value to their organizations. In our one case where a value-generating implementation journey started in the project management realm with Continuous/Convergent interventions and spread to the rest of the organization, senior executive and organizational level support was clearly evident.

Another important factor for successful implementation is recognizing the need to maintain a level of uncertainty with respect to the deployment of project management practices. Organizations that were continually able to derive value from their project management investments were those that maintained a respectful attitude toward project management and their ability to manage projects, but also continually tested their practice against externally sourced "best practice" guidelines, the experiences of other organizations (through benchmarking, etc.), and research developments in the field. These organizations were proud of their efforts to improve project management practice, and "owned" the implementation, but they also recognized the evolving nature of practice and welcomed uncertainty either in the environment or toward their practice. This recognition drove them to reflective practice, in which they learned from experience and continuous investment in improved practice. While management innovation might have been driven originally by perceived necessity, and was usually instigated at the senior-manager level, it continued because the project management team was never content to rest on its laurels, and project communities drove Continuous Convergent innovation over the long term.

Organizations that allowed themselves to believe their own, or others, marketing, and become certain about the "world-class" quality of their project management implementations, found that innovation activity ceased. This is clearly evident in those organizations that hired external help to implement "world-class" solutions: when the implementers left (either internal change agents or external consultants), they found their project management practice deteriorating rapidly. Within a relatively short period of time the implementation was judged by senior managers and/or clients as "failing," which led to Episodic interventions driven by senior managers, often Radical in nature. If these Episodic interventions were Convergent with existing project management models, they took on the nature of "fixes" and were unlikely in and of themselves to solve the problems with project management practice.

The process of innovation in project management is organic and evolving; there is no easily distinguishable end point. Even when reaching the polishing phase it is necessary to maintain capability by refining alignment and fit. Changes in organizational strategy may require the launch of a new cycle of innovation in circumstances where change needs more than maintenance if value is going to continue to be accessed through project management activity. Issues of "where you are" in the innovation life cycle, and sustainability of innovation, become important. Our cases suggest that formally recognizing an end to innovation is problematic, and eliminates the uncertainty necessary to drive continuous and ongoing innovation in management practice. Uncertainty is just as important to successful project management implementation as are sustained momentum and routinization: uncertainty provides the impetus for ongoing creative efforts of sense-making and social construction that can help to embed the practices in the fabric of organizational culture and become the foundation of management practice.

The greatest value can be derived from project management innovation by fitting the implementation to what may be changing in terms of context and strategy. This suggests that homogeneity or similarity between successful project management implementations should be more a coincidence than a given: homogeneity among project management implementations should not be expected.

Project management implementation, when it is recognized as a management innovation, entails fundamental change to existing management practices and belief systems. This level of organizational change impacts identity construction at many levels and in many departments in the organization. If the project management implementation is seen as simply the adoption of a technical tool, it is likely that these issues of identity construction will be ignored, and this in turn will hamper socialization, intergroup integration, and ultimately the embedding of the innovation in the fabric of the organization. Paying attention to intergroup safety (especially between departments and others affected by project management changes) is crucial to gaining the organization-wide acceptance and culture change that is supportive of the management innovation. For these reasons, successful project management implementation requires attention to issues of learning, socialization, routinization, contextual factors, role of power and history, labor processes, employee relationships, and organizational governance—issues more often associated with organizational change than with the adoption of new management technologies. Ignorance, or neglect, of these issues wastes implementation investment resources of all types. Recognizing these challenges requires project management implementation champions with not only technical expertise, but also the skills of political entrepreneurs.

An internal dynamics of continual transformation (as professed by organizational learning literature) should be treated as an organic issue of management innovation studies. According to Thompson and McHugh (2002), this particular aspect of the innovation process has been neglected in the literature, except in the literature on creativity. Our research monograph presents insights and propositions that could be a useful source of "added value" to the innovation debate. We do this by illustrating and interpreting the notion of internal dynamics of continual transition and transformation by means of identifying and analyzing the innovation journeys. Indeed, our research is grounded in the creativity discussion, as well as in the initial operational framework we borrowed from change literature.

Not every organization that innovates gets the positive benefits it is anticipating. Our empirical material indicates that project management implementation is the kind of innovation that is most often triggered by external pressures or requirements and environmental changes (globalization, public sector reforms, mergers, etc.) and sometimes by internal organizational initiatives to innovate with job or structure design. Sometimes innovations fail, often because underlying issues have not been sufficiently identified or triggers reveal only partial issues. Some innovations succeed initially, as they do address a prominent issue (they act like a bandage), and this is not necessarily a bad thing. The initial innovation can buy the organization time, and if it uses this time profitably, to attain a clear identification of real issues, subsequent innovations may be extremely effective. However, some initial successes ultimately lead to failure if they neglect to accommodate wider issues.

When a substantial innovation is exactly what the organization needs, a sustained process of innovation may not be required. However, we did not see many cases where this was true: in fact, only one case fits this description. In that situation, the organization began using project management as a management innovation in 1957 and did not innovate again until the late 1990s, and then stopped. In this organization, a culture of ongoing learning may in fact have meant that project management had become so much a part of the organization that it was no longer "innovation" for them to refine practice, but they are still sustaining innovation and gaining value from their actions.

On the whole, innovations are not squeezed into a short period of time: they continue over a period of years. The most active innovation in our study covered an eight-year period. One took place over 30 years, and over that time accomplished only two interventions. We believe that the organizations that have recorded the least time on their innovations are still actively participating in their journeys. The average innovation period was between two and nine years.

The most successful approach to innovation in project management is to consider it as a journey that requires a prolonged period of time to maintain and sustain the project management efficacy. Organizations that identified their project management implementations as "complete" failed to gain long-term benefits from their investments.

Organizations that succeeded with their innovations did so because each intervention became part of organizational culture. This constitutes adoption in its fullest form: through a process of socialization and routinization, the project management innovation is absorbed into normal working practice. Over time it is no longer regarded as innovative, but simply becomes part of the routine of the organizational operations.

In our study, we have refocused attention from the *management of innovation* to *implementing project management as a management innovation*. The question of "how" (in terms of a deeper analysis of journeys using the proposed conceptual frameworks) was as important to us as was the question of "what" has changed, or in which order changes have been made.

The trend for innovation is now (post-2000) less radical than it has been in the past (1980s and 1990s). The knowledge collected and circulated by professional bodies has led to "best practices" and "standards of practice" that guide both practice training and expectations as to what project management should entail, deliver, and realize in the form of benefits. From a managerial innovation perspective, we see that many of the organizations we looked at became quite conservative over time in their choices of both initial and follow-up interventions. While earlier journeys began very often with Radical intervention, innovation journeys that began in the last decade for the most part began, ended, and involved more Persistent innovation events. These were likely to build on existing models and to operate at the project management level in organizations, rather than the general management level. Organizations involved with these latter interventions continue to view project management as an operational rather than a strategic activity, and to improve on—rather than make significant breaks from—existing practice.

There was a group of organizations in our study that were driven by external forces (e.g., takeovers, mergers, project or business failures) to make quite radical innovations, often based on the adoption of a new project management approach and often involving strategic project management tools and techniques. Other organizations began their project management journeys through some sort of internal shakeup—often focused on improving project management throughput. Ultimately, however, almost all change journeys resulted in subsequent innovations that were based on improving and adapting existing project management practices. Persistent innovation events outnumbered other types of events considerably in the most recent years we studied.

Practical Implications

In our examination of 48 organizations, we found that no two project management implementations were identical and that similar innovation efforts in different contexts provided very different experiences. Designing a project management implementation for your organization will require careful assessment of: the context in which you operate; the specific strengths and/or barriers to project management and to the implementation of good projects that exist in your organization; and the benefits your organization would most value receiving from this implementation. Successful project management for your organization will not, and likely should not, be identical to that in other organizations, even when attempting the same type of innovation.

Every organization that sets out to introduce or improve project management must undertake four important activities. The first step is to determine where to invest its project management dollars. The second is to build a robust project management implementation that meets its needs. The third step is to introduce it in a way that makes it most acceptable to the organization. The fourth is to identify what to measure to make sure that the investment is paying off.

This study illustrates different types of project management innovation journeys and the outcomes of these journeys. The insights into what types of implementations fit successfully within organizations operating in different contexts, and insights into the benefits and values organizations are receiving from these implementations, should allow project managers to recognize different strategies for their own purposes.

The guidelines below draw from these empirical findings to provide food for thought for organizations as to how they may best go about shaping project management implementations to obtain maximum benefit. Our research provides further evidence of the importance of executive-level support and buy-in to the success of implementation of project management. Executive management needs to understand and support the implementation of project management innovations, and more specifically must play an active role in developing approaches to deal with intergroup safety and socialization of the new practices at all levels across the organization. Project management associations need to continue to engage with executive levels and perhaps agitate to have project management added to the management curriculum, in order to help managers recognize that project management is not a technology or tool but a management practice that impacts many other aspects of management (such as culture, motivation, identity construction, intergroup safety and innovation), and is in turn impacted by them.

A fundamental message that emerges from this research is that project management implementation is a management innovation generating significant organizational change, and to be successful, it needs the full support and participation of senior levels of management. It is also important to recognize that project management implementation is a group activity, the success of which also depends on group processes such as intergroup safety, reflexivity, participatory decision-making, collective learning, socialization, and routinization. Literature that relates to the management of management innovation and organizational change provides insights into the socio-political and behavioral considerations that require attention in this regard.

Project management implementation journeys need to be viewed as ongoing operational activities—to be seen more as continuous improvement activities than as projects with set budgets and start and stop deadlines. That said, changing circumstances—and, in particular, changes in key actors—will trigger more episodic interventions. This research suggests that the organizations that recognize project management as a strategic asset at the executive level are much more likely to gain valuable benefits from their project management investments and supports further research on this topic.

At the same time, research shows that senior executives are only likely to be interested in project implementation when there is a sense of urgency; therefore, Episodic innovations are more likely to get executive attention. This means that project management professionals need to be ready to deal with the executives as trusted advisors when an external trigger activates executive interest. Building relationships and understanding organizational context is not something that can be done quickly but needs ongoing investment. Professional networks that embed project management in managerial thinking in organizations prepare the way for future innovation. Recognizing that expertise in project management is not the number one criterion for championing project management innovation is another important consideration. Strategies to gain buy-in at all levels of the organization are fundamentally important and ultimately more important than change leadership or executive support, because even highly successful innovations that are not embedded in practice cease as soon as that leadership is no longer present. Awareness of the various types of project management innovation journey types involved in project management implementation can inform planning and management of innovation.

Guidance for Practice

Whether you like to start from a point of success or failure, it is clear from this research that innovating the management of projects requires organizations to first seek the right innovation before focusing on doing the innovation right.

From a success perspective, by examining the experience of organizations innovating their project management, we can see that organizations that innovate successfully do so because they select the right innovation and then go on to tailor it to meet organizational, business, and operational needs, yielding ongoing benefits.

Likewise, there is evidence of three situations where innovations are unsuccessful. The first is failing to select the right innovation. The second and third are instances where the innovation doesn't become part of the organizational culture because of socio-organizational behavioral challenges: rejection by the organization because the innovation doesn't fulfill organizational needs, even if it does meet the needs of the practitioners, or rejection of the innovation by practitioners who can't make it fit their work routines.

Step 1. Do the Right Innovation Event

Our first recommendation is to deal with current needs first. If you have an intense need to do something immediately to deal with or to avert imminent catastrophe, we suggest that you address your immediate concerns before you consider investing in a significant project management implementation. Deal with urgent issues immediately. Put a bandage on them if you must, but do not make an investment decision based on the current crisis. In many instances, this situation is when project management first comes to the attention of senior management. It is absolutely critical in innovating that you make sure you are addressing the root causes of your discomfort, and not solely the symptoms or the issues that are most top-of-mind because of the current crisis. Our best advice is to hire some expert project managers (either internally or through a consulting agency) to address the specific concerns that you are facing immediately.

Our second recommendation is that, the crisis having been dealt with, you then take the time to conduct a complete assessment of your situation in order to identify the right initial innovation. As the initial innovation is often the most radical, and sets the direction for subsequent interventions, it is important to identify the right initial innovation. Throughout this monograph we provide significant insights into what types of innovation events fit successfully within organizations operating in different contexts, and the benefits and values organizations are receiving from these implementations today. A clear intent is a good place to start for success. The less ambiguous the trigger (think mandated vs. generic best practice), the clearer the strategic relationship of the innovation to the organization—and the clearer the realization why this innovation is necessary to everyone within the organization, not just those directly involved. This should be closely followed by an assessment of the organizational capacity for change, including its willingness, its ownership, and its capability.

Key Considerations

- o Immediate existing crises must be handled so that the real issues can be identified, allowing time for creativity in innovation.
- o The innovation selected must match the needs of the organization. The selected innovation must clearly identify the meaningful anticipated benefits and set an unambiguous intent.
- o Executive power should be applied in the sponsorship of the innovation.

Step 2. Do the Innovation Right

Successful management innovation is a complex process that requires an inclusive process whereby creative involvement increases ownership of, and commitment to, the changes in practice. The interplay of identities and interests at work must be incorporated in the way innovation is managed, to facilitate cooperative engagement in the process. Widespread adoption requires legitimization by executives, and it also requires ground-level buy-in. Apparently successful innovations that have not been embedded in the fabric of organizational practice will fail when leadership is no longer present (innovation "ends" and leader leaves—retires, has a baby, etc.). Resistance met in the past will return in the future if it is not resolved adequately. Some useful resolution skills include: group integration; inclusive decision-making processes; and creation of ownership or commitment in those with concerns. Note that the trigger for each innovation event may not be the root problem, and further interventions may be required to solve issues successfully enough to generate real value from the project management innovation in the long term. This is why it is important to consider project management innovation as a journey.

The following guidelines draw from our empirical findings to provide factors to be considered in deciding how to go about innovating project management implementations to obtain anticipated benefits.

Key Considerations

- • Secure executive and senior management sponsorship and support. Executive and senior management support helps set a clear organizational intent for the innovation.
- o There must be strong authority behind the leadership of the management innovation.
- o Championed support creates organizational buy-in.

Note that the first trigger is most often an external trigger or crisis, and the strength of this initial trigger is important in gaining suitable sponsorship.

- Create innovation championship and implementation leadership. Important factors include development of suitable:
  o Leadership of the interventions in the innovation journey to ensure that the interventions are managed correctly
  o Championing by leader and executive to facilitate organizational buy-in
  o Socio-political skills, so that the innovation is understood at all level of the organization and ownership is created

Note that championship and leadership are even more crucial if executive sponsorship is missing, as the champion/leader must adopt the role of political entrepreneur.

- Develop social context for innovation and change:
  o Build a realistic understanding of your organizational capacity for change, including its willingness, its ownership and capability.
  o Establish strategies to ensure buy-in and ownership for the innovation.
  o Establish that there is sufficient credibility and legitimacy for the innovation to be implemented.
  o Create an understanding that project management innovations result in changes in the way people work. They create organizational change and are not simply a new tool.
- Understand that innovation is a journey that cycles through four stages, one or many times.
  o Chose each subsequent intervention to respond to the reality of the issues experienced by the organization.
  o Respond to a specific problem or problems in an appropriate way; don't assume "best practice" will resolve these issues.
  o Remain flexible to the inevitable changes resulting from the innovation.
  o Adapt through tailoring and pruning. It is socialization and tailoring of the innovation that gives it value. These efforts promote buy-in and realization of benefits and give the innovation a chance of being maintained and sustained.
  o Use uncertainty as a trigger that provides impetus for ongoing creative efforts.
  o Be ready to cycle around the innovation process again in response to changes in organizational and external situations.

Research Implications

This research contributes to two important bodies of literature: management innovation and project management. By closely observing differences across organizations in what they implement for one particular management innovation— project management implementation—we contribute to the study of management innovation. We provide further evidence of the contextual, socially constructed nature of management practices, and the need for careful identification of truly comparative distinguishing features before attempting to generalize "best practices." Applying management innovation theories to the study of project management implementations contributes to our understanding of the process of improving project management practice. Starting from a population of organizations whose primary similarity was that all were interested in addressing the challenge of managing projects, and then by carefully identifying the distinguishing characteristics of how the implementation of project management was influenced by different contextual, socio-political, and behavioral factors, we provide a foundation for recognizing distinct types of innovation journeys that face a range of different challenges in accomplishing the same organizational goal. By illustrating the different project management innovation journeys that are implemented in various organizations under the explicit desire to improve the practice of project management, we illustrate the plasticity of management innovation, and identify some of the factors that influence which elements of the rhetoric are adopted in different contexts. While each of the innovation journeys examined in this study is unique, we highlight similarities in the patterns of innovation events, environmental factors, triggers, and types of support across innovation journeys in ways that will help organizations beginning an innovation journey to assess their own situations. By studying examples, they will be able to identify appropriate strategies for managing their own management innovation processes.

Contributions to Theory

We have provided a theoretical foundation for the study of project management as a management innovation. We have also provided a review of management innovation concepts and theories as a foundation for an emerging research agenda exploring organizational project management.

The dynamics of how management innovations are implemented are poorly explored in extant management innovation literature. Most of this literature looks at a generic measure of innovation across many types of management innovation at one point in time. Based on concepts from management innovation theory, and an initial operational framework from the change literature, the current study adds to scholarly understanding of management innovation implementation by focusing attention on management innovation as a journey. In this exploration, we emphasized the key role of both context and individuals in shaping these journeys, and identified the key constructs (specifically, innovation events involving triggers, actions, and outcomes, linked in an intentional and responsive manner into innovation journeys) that are necessary for developing theory relating to the dynamics of management innovation. While the journey types were identified from data that explicitly focused on one type of innovation, we believe that testing of these propositions will support them as important aspects of all management innovation journeys.

Implementation of project management in the existing project management literature is typically described in a stepwise fashion that is associated with: the adoption of "best practices"; internal assessment; benchmarking against other organizations; and continuous improvement (often involving more strategic project management governance). However, evidence presented here suggests that successful implementation of project management requires a much more nuanced and sophisticated understanding of organizational power, politics, inter-relationships, and change.

This study contributes to our understanding of the interfaces between general management and project management. We show that the emphasis on technical rationality that is embedded in more standardized and detailed analytical models and methods is misplaced when it comes to addressing the gap in our understanding of how to successfully implement project management. This study suggests that project management theory must explore the role of uncertainty in facilitating innovation. It must address the issue of the paradox of trying to minimize uncertainty while still allowing enough of it to persist to support innovations in management practice.

Contributions to Methodology

We developed a model for representing innovation events and innovation journeys that helps us to deal with large amounts of data and make meaningful comparisons across organizations. This research demonstrates the usefulness of the model by Street and Gallupe (2009) for operationalizing the types of innovation events that make up an innovation implementation journey. Adoption of this model across the discipline will provide a solid foundation that ensures effectiveness and rigor in cross-case comparisons of project management implementation and other managerial innovation events.

We illustrated the problems associated with using cross-sectional, cross-industry, survey-based research methods to attempt to understand management innovation. Survey information that lacks the context to interpret it can easily lead to faulty conclusions. By collecting a large sample of detailed case studies of one particular type of management innovation journey across organizations, industries, and time, we provided solid evidence of the fundamental importance of specific unique elements of innovation dynamics in the interpretation of findings in this complex area of practice. One case in point: in a survey-based study conducted at one point in time, Case 63 would have lived on in the literature as an example of the "textbook" method for successfully implementing project management by beginning at the project level and moving up through maturity levels to the enterprise-wide strategic office. Our ability to extend the study over time showed that this case actually provided evidence of a different nature: it demonstrated the importance of having a project change champion to initiate and motivate change while also illustrating the problems inherent in this approach, as organizational members tend to rely on this person and not engage in the more difficult and reflective practice of embedding these changes in the identity construction of themselves and their employees. Our investigation showed that the latter step is crucial to the ongoing sustainability of an innovation, and to ongoing innovation.

We highlighted the importance of going beyond coding of case data into innovation events and journeys to include a final step: that of returning to the detail to determine whether journeys that appear similar in terms of types of innovation events actually deliver similar outcomes.

Limitations of the Research

All research is limited in some way, and this leaves the door open for future and more pointed studies to address these limitations. The primary limitations in this work are based on the case data source. First, there is a potential positive bias toward project management inherent in this database. Organizations participating in this study were largely interested in improving project management and, in many cases, extremely effective in both implementing and practicing project management. As such, these organizations possibly represent a biased sample, in that they may be both more prone to invest in project management and more likely to be successful in selecting the right interventions and modifications to industry practice. A mitigating factor is that we did come across several unsuccessful innovation journeys in this data, despite this bias.

Second, the research draws heavily on a case study database that was collected for another purpose. There were times when meaningful research questions could not be pursued because the needed data was not available in this data set. On three occasions we rectified this lack by conducting additional interviews. However, the fact remains that purpose-collected data may provide more specific assessment of some of the innovation constructs than was possible with this data set.

Finally, any collected data ages more rapidly than analysis can be written up. In regard to the data for this study, at the time of our investigation it had been four to six years since the bulk of the case data had been collected. There was a possibility that changes in the business culture or environment, such as the financial crisis over the intervening years, may have changed some organizations' approaches to implementing project management. However, this data reports on project management implementations occurring over a 30-year period, reflecting many such environmental changes, and so this risk is reduced somewhat for this particular study and data set. In addition, more and more organizations implementing project management in the later stages of our data collection period demonstrated a decided tendency to implement "packaged" project management constructs, and if anything, the financial crisis likely increased this trend, due to the increased urgency to improve practice and minimize risk.

Directions for Future Research

One of the often frustrating results of most research was also true of this project: for every question we answered, we identified at least one further question that needed to be addressed. This section discusses the key areas of future research we believe are raised by our study—in effect laying out an agenda for needed research to take this study forward and further develop our understanding of project management as a management innovation.

Our most significant contribution to the theory and methods of the study of management innovation may be the naming of the varieties of journey types. Future research adopting our operationalization of management innovation events will extend and test the usefulness of this model, contribute to building more coherence across cases and studies, and help deepen our understanding of the mechanics of management innovation.

One finding of this study is that project management innovation efforts may be more conservative today than earlier due to increasing demands on organizations to maintain a competitive advantage. This need to focus on business rather than on internal process will more commonly call for Persistent interventions than for widespread changes across the entire organization, which will change the way the management of project-based work is carried out. This increased conservatism toward the use of professional standardization may be evidence that much of today's management cohort takes it for granted that standardized practice is preferable to creative, context-dependent problem-solving. The question here is: Does the literature lead practice or follow it? Organizations may adopt existing theory and best practice and advice, or they may chose to lead theory development by making practice choices that challenge the use of existing theory. Clearer answers may be forthcoming when, in future work, we consider what type of intervention and innovation is applied to project-based work in a harsher economic climate. The small conservative tweaks of a Persistent approach may no longer provide a suitable response to business needs; it will be interesting to see if some organizations become more radical in their approaches to gaining value from project management. Future and longitudinal research is necessary to confirm this hypothesis and explore the reasons for it more deeply.

The country cultural implications of appropriate project management implementations need to be further explored, especially with respect to cultural impacts on the processes of socialization, routinization, and learning. We identified what we believe to be some cultural influences on both what is implemented and how well it is embedded in the receiving organization; however, country culture was not a focus of this study, and our data set provided us with only minimal data to help us explore this question. Based on our findings, however, this does appear to be a fruitful area for further research.

Several of the cases in our data set provided us with insight into Radical change that was unintended, emergent, and relatively slow. These particular journeys were less easily classified as management innovation, because by definition, management innovation requires intentional action. Further analysis of these cases using a complexity theory perspective will likely provide valuable insight into the dynamic interaction of events over time. Complexity-based analysis will examine in detail implications of complex adaptive methods of relating (Cicmil, Cooke-Davies, Crawford,

& Richardson, 2009) or the initiating conditions, far from equilibrium state, deviation amplification, and fractal patterns and scalability (Plowman et al., 2007).

The impact of the "guru" and the professional association on the construction of the artifacts and power knowledge surrounding project management must be examined critically with respect to project management implementation journeys. These two actors in the project management world have the capacity to (re)constitute our collective understanding not only of project management but also of reality and our sense of self in respect to management innovation. Understanding the role of these actors in this innovation effort is critical if we are to fully understand how innovation happens. By presenting a unified account of management that obscures the realities of organizing and managing, gurus seek to redefine and reconstruct the "management of business" and the "business of management" by obscuring the complicated reality that the future of management practice will always be a surprise. Our research provides some evidence that the efforts of the project management industry (including gurus, professional associations, consultants, and trainers) to reduce uncertainty or at least reduce the perception of uncertainty in selling project management implementations may in fact be planting the seed for failed innovation attempts. Other researchers, starting with Shenhar and Dvir (1996), have shown that one size of project management does not fit all. This research suggests that there is both an increasing tendency to provide, and to look for, a "certified" solution, while evidence suggests that this is not a successful approach. Further research is necessary to test this proposition and possibly to develop research evidence from which to show that the straightforward, technically rational, "guru"-led benefits of project management innovation are not well suited to the majority of organizational milieus, and that mindful consideration of specific project management situations is essential to the development of appropriate project management interventions and innovations. In addition, we will need to develop practitioners capable of the mindful consideration and consumption of research and consultant literature necessary in order to accurately diagnose project management challenges and develop context-sensitive solutions.

Other areas ripe for future study include the nature and role of legitimizing rhetoric in "selling" project management. Preoccupation with dramatic moves and maneuvers that "sell" may create false expectations around the "creation of value." The act of legitimizing rhetoric creates false expectations or obscures power conflicts and impacts; the impact of these "whitewashing" activities are likely to be very negative. Examination of the motivation for the organization's investments in project management, and how these arguments and the participants in the legitimization process are held accountable, are areas for fertile discussion.

Final Remarks

We would like to underline several things that we as a community—including practitioners and researchers—must do to improve the success of project management innovations.

First, practitioners need to be aware of the social contexts embedded in power structures supported by political aspirations and individual life choices that do not necessarily align with the assumptions that are taken for granted, and which privilege goals of efficiency over business effectiveness. Second, the research community needs to develop better evidence and tools to help practitioners diagnose the conditions that may be supportive or inimical to project management implementation. Third, we need to develop an understanding of the project management professional competencies necessary to understand and steer project management innovations with due respect to the social life of organizations.

As with all research, the final judge of the usefulness of this study is left to you, the readers. We hope that all experienced researchers and practitioners can recognize patterns from organizations they know in the detailed case narratives provided, and learn from our discussions of management innovation theory. In reviewing these results with practitioners and academics around the world, we have heard that they hold strong face validity for our chosen audience and provide tools that are useful in diagnosing and recommending appropriate project management implementations for a variety of organizations. We hope you find these results useful.

Finally, we would like to express our appreciation to the researchers who collected the case data we used in this study, and to PMI for supporting the original Researching the Value of Project Management project. Without this support and effort, a study of this nature would not be possible.

Appendix

Case Descriptions for Selected Data Set (Adapted from Thomas and Mullaly, PMI (2008), Appendix A)

Case 23

Based in China and operating nationally from Shanghai, this organization carries out work in the IT sector. The IT Business Unit is responsible for IT projects, undertaking mainly customer-driven project work.

Originating as an entrepreneurial pioneering start-up approximately 10 years before the research study, this organization has a state ownership structure. It is a leading provider for software and financial processing solutions in China. Although it does not have any strong competitors at this time it is thought to be highly competitive. The predominant culture in this organization is entrepreneurial, customer- and investor-focused; success and failure are both tolerated.

Project Management Culture

Project management has been a part of this organization since 1999 and is moderately mature. This is a project-based organization—almost every person in the company was involved in the project management improvement.

Project management is valued throughout the IT Business Unit, with project management influencing their corporate culture. By increasing project management capabilities (specifically in improved ability to control risk and allocate resources), the whole team's potential was tapped into, which induced positive influence to the culture formulation under the competitive environment and was reflected in benefit allocation. Project managers experienced improved customer satisfaction, senior management reported greater transparency.

Researchers observed the project management to be fairly effective, noting some aspects of project management implementation to be beyond compare: e.g., client satisfaction, effective communication, project transparency, risk control process management, document management, and cost control.

Table A1. The Benefits Case 23 Experienced from Project Management

Tangible	Intangible
Customer retention	Greater social good
Increased customer share	More effective human resources
	Improved corporate culture

Case 25

This organization is the largest IT public sector provider in Denmark, with 60% of the market share. It has several international competitors, one of which it also partners with. Competition was moderate at the time of study and is expected to increase. The IT projects it undertakes are mainly customer-driven project work. The predominant culture in this organization is innovative and competitive.

Project Management Culture

Project management has been a part of this organization since 1980, is moderately mature, and is generally well respected. Over the period 2004–2007, a new project management model was developed, allowing for multiple project programs for customers.

The project management model provides a common frame of reference in this organization, allowing a uniform approach to the processes, methods, instruments, attitudes, and behavior for managing their projects. The implementation was put in place to cope with the challenges of managing a program of projects. Project managers reported that there was good cross-project communication and that there was both employee and customer satisfaction. Better satisfaction has led to a better project culture including time management, internal engagement and ownership. One of this organization's project managers was awarded "Project Manager of the Year" in 2007. Clearer project objectives, improved delivery, and reduced project failure were also reported in this organization.

Researchers observed that the common frame of reference was fully adopted by the organization and had grown to be the project management's own. The researchers noted that project managers express a multi-faceted view on project management: it is a well-developed basis of tools, methods, and well-defined roles of the project organization, and management support gives focus on leadership more than on project control.

Table A2. The Benefits Case 25 Experienced from Project Management

Tangible	Intangible
Reduced write-offs and rework	Improved competitiveness
	Attainment of strategic objectives
	New product/service streams
	More effective human resources
	Improved reputation
	Improved overall management
	Improved corporate culture

Case 34

Based in the UK and operating nationally and internationally, this organization carries out work in the very highly competitive education sector. The data covers strategic change projects, as this organization undertakes mainly internal-driven project work; however, the organization as a whole does also undertake customer-driven projects. Competition in this sector is also complex, based on a number of factors such as price, resource, quality, and reputation. The predominant culture in this organization is innovative, customer- and stakeholder-focused.

Project Management Culture

Project management has been a part of this organization since the 1990s; however, it has low project management maturity. In 2006 this organization moved to using PRINCE2 to facilitate formal control, visibility, and promotion of a series of interlinked projects.

There is divided opinion between the administration and many of the academic employees regarding the use of centralized formal project management. Project management is perceived by some to effectively align business cases with the organization's strategy and to create process alignment, allowing for: confidence in timely project completion; efficient use of resources and justification of project plans; and improved cross-organizational horizontal and vertical communication. This view is not shared by all.

The researchers observed value in terms of process alignment and noted that project management could play an important role in an effective and efficient delivery of the university's strategic initiatives.

Table A3. The Benefits Case 34 Experienced from Project Management

Tangible	Intangible
	Attainment of strategic objectives
	Improved overall management
	Improved corporate culture

Case 35

Based in Beijing, this national Chinese construction organization is responsible for construction projects, undertaking mainly customer-driven project work. It is in the top 20 of China's largest construction organizations. Competition in this sector is fierce and well regulated. This organization has a state ownership structure and is regarded by this research team as a highly competitively placed organization. The predominant culture in this organization is customer- and investor-focused. This organization has a heavy project management implementation.

Project Management Culture

Project management has been a part of this organization since the mid-1990s and is very mature. In this organization, project management innovation was implemented as a result of an external motivation: government regulations and world best practices. Project management is well respected in this organization. The original innovation has been adopted fully by the organization, with the most recent innovations adapting it to fit the organization itself. The most recent project management improvement implemented by this organization, in 2006, was a lessons learned casebook publication. Focus on quality and safety, human resource quality and safety has improved employee and organization project management capability.

The full adoption of project management as an innovation is realized for this organization in many ways. The project managers view the management systems and processes as aiding better management, control, and delivery of a project according to the contract and to the customer's satisfaction. This has lead to quality improvements, good reputation in the industry, and enterprise-wide thinking.

The researchers of this case observed that this organization has successfully established its economic enterprise management system and has built good reputation in the industry.

Table A4. The Benefits Case 34 Experienced from Project Management

Tangible	Intangible
	Improved competitiveness
	Improved quality of life
	More effective human resources
	Improved reputation
	Improved overall management
	Improved corporate culture
	Improved regulatory compliance

Case 43

Operating regionally in Queensland, Australia, this organization carries out public-sector project work for the government.

This organization is assessed to be moderately competitive; although competition for projects is low, there is a high level of competition with the private sector for resources (both staff and materials). The predominant culture in this organization is innovative with a focus on customers and stakeholders.

Project Management Culture

Project management has been a part of this organization since 1990 and is moderately mature. Project management is central to the organization's existence, as success in projects is fundamental to its business. A cooperative view to project management exists in the organization, and researchers noted that customer and stakeholder satisfaction is high; many projects are delivered on time, on budget and with extremely high quality. The innovation of a Project Manager Management Unit was put in place to provide support for use and understanding of a project management framework.

The project teams reported that there have been improvements in risk management, coaching and training, and program management. Scope has been managed to an increasing degree, resulting in measurably fewer incidences of scope creep in recent projects.

Table A5. The Benefits Case 43 Experienced from Project Management

Tangible	Intangible
	Improved competitiveness
	Attainment of strategic objectives
	More effective human resources
	Improved corporate culture

Case 47

A multinational based in the UK, this organization carries out work in the defense and aerospace sector. The standalone project business unit is responsible for engineering projects, undertaking mainly customer- and product-driven project work.

This organization has a widely held ownership structure, working in a global industry and providing service to governments worldwide. The predominant culture in this organization is customer- and stakeholder-focused.

Project Management Culture

Project management has been a part of this organization since 1996 and has a low level of maturity. The status of project management in this organization is determined by a complex relationship between this organization and their client. This organization cooperates with project management in a dismissive manner. A flawed project management model was eventually augmented by the local and client management with earned value reporting. The organization reported satisfaction with the innovation; however, the case researchers noted that actual tools and techniques that were focused on (i.e., earned value in particular) have had very little impact on the management of the project, as evidenced by the continued failure to meet either schedule or budget targets. The implementation was put in place to increase client perception of project control and management. Researchers suggest the "failure to improve the project management practice even with significant investment in consulting, training and procedures, is likely attributable to the fact that the changes made have only paid lip service to the problems running rampant in the organization with respect to the underlying motivations of the parties involved, the dominant techno culture."

Table A6. The Benefits Case 43 Experienced from Project Management

Tangible	Intangible
Revenue increases	Improved reputation
Customer retention	
Increased customer share	
Greater market share	
Reduced write-offs and rework	

Case 52

Case 52 is an international pharmaceutical organization operating from Copenhagen, Denmark. The Supply Operations & Engineering department is responsible for production and logistics projects, undertaking mainly product-driven project work. This organization has a widely held ownership structure. It is facing a major competitive challenge that will impact in the next four to six years. The predominant culture in this organization is strongly professional, with some silos of knowledge.

Project Management Culture

Project management has been a part of this organization since the 1990s, and is low to moderate in maturity. Project management is respected in the organization. A project management method was put in place to strengthen interaction between a larger number of projects with higher complexity. After this innovation the project teams reported satisfaction in their working: "The toolbox provides freedom, but it is also something that you can lean on and find the [resource] you need." The cases researchers agreed, observing that projects are done with enough resource and benefits are achieved. There is a career path and project management has top management attention.

Table A7. The Benefits Case 52 Experienced from Project Management

Tangible	Intangible
	Attainment of strategic objectives
	More effective human resources
	Improved corporate culture

Case 63

Operating across western Canada, this organization carries out work in the energy sector. The IT PMO is responsible for IT projects, undertaking mainly internally driven project work.

This organization has an income trust ownership structure and operates within a competitive environment of rapid growth and unpredictable demand. Operating many lines of business, competitors in one line can be customers or partners in other lines. Competition is friendly and collaborative, yet intense and complex. The predominant culture in this organization is one of growth and entrepreneurship.

Project Management Culture

Project management has been a part of this organization since 1994 and is moderately mature. A cooperative to respected view of project management exists within this organization. This organization has employed a formal project management system, culminating in a strong PMO with an aim to formalize project management structure and processes, and as such, improve project management competency within the organization. Project managers reported being "given IT increased credibility and confidence from senior executives. The project management implementation has improved communication, commitment, accountability and focus, especially in the IT department." The implementation fits strategy and is formal but grounded in a project management framework. The CEO directly associated the organization's ability to be successful in the future with project management capabilities in the organization. He stated that every penny spent in project management has been a good investment. Even in an organization founded by accountants and largely focused on finance and controls, the expenditure on project management is seen as essential.

Table A8. The Benefits Case 63 Experienced from Project Management

Tangible	Intangible
Revenue increases	Attainment of strategic objectives
Reduced write-offs and rework	More effective human resources
	Improved overall management
	Improved corporate culture
	Improved regulatory compliance

At the time of the PMO innovation the case researcher noted there was better alignment and accomplishment of strategy. Communication had improved—project management processes helped disseminate information and helps overcome blocks that occur between business units. There was decreased churn in projects (less wasted resources) because of a more comprehensive start, and things don't get overlooked.

Since these benefits were identified, a case update shows the devolvement of the PMO due to a change in staffing and strategic focus.

Case 72

This construction organization operating from the Sichuan province of southwest China carries out projects in the energy sector. This organization has a state ownership structure. The large-scale nature of the projects contracted to this organization means it has little competitive pressure over the next 10 to 20 years.

Project Management Culture

Project management has been a part of this organization since 1998–1991; due to legal requirements, this organization cannot get funding without project management. A respected view of project management exists within the organization. It is project-oriented and has become well known for its advanced project management. It has a full set of management methods, processes, and templates for planning, controlling, and governing various aspects of a project throughout its whole life cycle. Project managers specifically see the use of competitive bidding process as valuable for selecting competent contractors with the lowest price, and the tender documents and contract provide valuable bases for management of payment and changes.

Recent innovations focus on multi-project management; project management training, self-learning and PMP certification; and effective management of research projects. The current project management implementation is thought to be well suited for this organization at this time, with the organization having strong brand awareness and additional government contracts.

Table A9. The Benefits Case 72 Experienced from Project Management

Tangible	Intangible
Revenue increases	Attainment of strategic objectives
Customer retention	Greater social good
Increased customer share	More effective human resources
	Improved reputation
	Improved overall management
	Improved corporate culture
	Improved regulatory compliance

Case 75

A Canadian-based North American multinational, this organization carries out work in the energy sector. The IT PMO is responsible for IT projects. This organization has a widely held ownership structure. Parts of this organization's business are highly regulated. It operates in a competitive environment of rapid growth and unpredictable demand. It has competition for customers and partners, which is friendly and collaborative yet intense and complex. At the time of data capture the predominant culture in this organization is in transition, with some silos of quite different culture.

Project Management Culture

Project management has been a part of this organization since 1999 and it is moderately mature. It is recognized that project-based work is fundamental to this organization. With initial strong leadership in project management, this organization ran a center of excellence in project management. The Center of Excellence resulted in significant annual savings. With staffing changes the role of the PMO began changing. The organization has a mixed attitude to project management.

A redefinition of the PMO from a methodology/support PMO to a delivery PMO was put in place to improve project performance and to enforce adherence to procedures and processes. The project management of this organization, "a fast follower" and risk-averse, addresses associated concerns by giving confidence of success. The case researchers also noted that the organization had better control and predictability of costs, which directly affected its bottom line in the regulated side of its business, and gave the organization greater confidence to expand, for example, through acquisitions and development of capital assets—which is accomplished through projects.

Table A10. The Benefits Case 72 Experienced from Project Management

Tangible	Intangible
Cost savings	Attainment of strategic objectives
Revenue increases	Improved quality of life
	More effective human resources
	Improved reputation
	Improved regulatory compliance

References

Abrahamson, E. (1991). Managerial fads and fashions: The diffusion and rejection of innovations. *Academy of Management Review, 16(3),* 586–612.

Abrahamson, E. (1996). Management fashion. *Academy of Management Review, 21(1),* 254–285.

Adams, R., Bessant, J., & Phelps, R. (2006). Innovation management measurement: A review. *International Journal of Management Review 8(1),* 21–47.

Andersen, E. (2008). *Project management—An organizational perspective.* London, UK: Prentice-Hall.

Anderson, N. R., & King, N. (1993). Innovation in organisations. In C. L. Cooper & I. T. Robertson (Eds.), *International review of industrial and organisational psychology* (Vol. 8). Chichester, England: Wiley.

Andersen, E. S., & Vaagaasar, A. L. (2009, March). Project management improvement efforts—Creating project management value by uniqueness or mainstream thinking? *Project Management Journal, 40*(1) (Special Edition).

Armour, H. O., & Teece, D. J. (1980). Vertical integration and technological innovation. *Review of Economics and Statistics, 62,* 470–474.

Benders, J., & Van Veen, S. (2003). What's in a fashion? Interpretive viability and management fashions. *Organization, 8(1),* 33–53.

Birkinshaw, J., & Mol, M. J. (2006) How management innovation happens. *MIT Sloan Management Review, 47(4),* 81–88.

Birkinshaw, J., Hamel, G., & Mol, M. J. (2008). Management innovation. *Academy of Management Review, 33(4),* 825–845.

Boddy, D., & Buchanan, D. (1992). Who has an interest? In D. Boddy & D. Buchanan, *Take the lead: Interpersonal skills of project manager,* (pp. 55–70). London, UK: Prentice Hall International.

Boer, H., & During, W. E. (2001). Innovation, what innovation? A comparison between product, process, and organizational innovation. *International Journal of Technology Management, 22(1),* 83–107.

Blomquist, T., Hallgren, M., Nilsson, A., & Soderholm, A. (2010). Project-as-practice: In search of project management research that matters. *Project Management Journal, 41*(1), 5–16.

Brady, T., & Maylor, H. (2010). The improvement paradox in project contexts: A clue to the way forward? *International Journal of Project Management, 28*(8), 787–795.

Buchanan, D., & Badham, R. (1999). *Power, politics, and organisational change: Winning the turf game* (pp. 166–168, 185–189). London, England: SAGE.

Burnes, B. (2004). *Managing change: A strategic approach to organizational dynamics.* London, England: Prentice Hall.

Caldwell, R. (2003). Models of change agency: A fourfold classification. *British Journal of Management, 14(2),* 131–142.

Chapman, M. (1997). Preface: Social anthropology, business studies, and cultural issues. *International Studies in Management & Organization, 26*(4), 3–29.

Cicmil, S., & Hodgson, D. (2006). Critical research in project management— An introduction. In D. Hodgson & S. Cicmil (Eds.), *Making projects critical* (pp. 1–28). Basingstoke, UK and New York, NY: Palgrave McMillan.

Cicmil, S., Cooke-Davies, T., Crawford, L., & Richardson, K. (2009). Exploring the complexity of projects: Implications of complexity theory for project management practice (Research Monograph). Newtown Square, PA: PMI.

Cicmil, S., Hodgson, D., Lindgren, M., & Packendorff, J. (2009). Project management behind the façade. *Ephemera: theory & politics in organization, 9*(2), 78–92.

Cicmil, S., & Braddon, D. (2012, in press). Fading glory? Decision-making around the project—How and why "glory" projects fail. In T. Williams & K. Samset (Eds.), *Project governance—Getting investments right.* London, UK: Palgrave.

Cicmil, S., Dordevic, Z., & Zivanovic, S. (2009). Understanding the adoption of project management in Serbian organizations: Insights from a exploratory study. *Project Management Journal, 40*(1) (Special Edition).

Cohen, M. D., March, J. G., & Olsen, J. P. (1972). A garbage can model of organizational choice. *Administrative Science Quarterly, 17*(1), 1–25.

Cooke-Davies, T. J., Crawford, L. H., & Lechler, T. G. (2009). Project management systems: Moving project management from an operational to strategic discipline. *Project Management Journal, 40*(1) (Special Edition).

Crawford, L. H., & Helm, J. (2009). Government and governance: The value of project management in the public sector. *Project Management Journal, 40*(1) (Special Edition).

Czarniawska-Joerges, B., & Sevon, G. (1996). *Translating organizational change.* Berlin, Germany: Walter De Gryter.

Daft, R. L. (1978). A dual-core model of organizational innovation. *Academy of Management Journal, 21(2)* 193–210.

Damanpour, F. (1987). The adoption of technological, administrative, and ancillary innovations: Impact of organizational factors. *Journal of Management, 13(4),* 675–688.

Damanpour, F. (1991). Organizational innovation: A meta analysis of determinants and moderators. *Academy of Management Journal, 34*(3), 555–590.

Damanpour, F., & Evan, W. M. (1984). Organizational innovation and performance: The problem of organizational lag. *Administrative Science Quarterly 29,* 392–409.

Damanpour, F., & Schneider, M. (2006). Phases of the adoption of innovation in organizations: Effects of environment, organization, and top managers. *British Journal of Management, 17(3),* 215–236.

Damanpour, F., Walker, R. M., & Avellaneda, C. N. (2009). Combinative effects of innovation types on organizational performance: A longitudinal study of public services. *Journal of Management Studies, 46(4)*, 650–675.

Dewett, T., Whittier, N. C., & Williams, S. D. (2007). Internal diffusion: The conceptualizing innovation implementation. *Competitiveness Review, 17*(1/2), 8–25.

DiMaggio, P., & Powell, W. (1983). The iron cage revisited: Institutional isomorphism and collective rationality in organizational fields. *American Sociological Review, 48*, 147–160.

Dosi, G. (1988). Sources, procedures, and microeconomic effects of innovation. *Journal of Economic Literature, 26*, 1120–1171.

Dougherty, D. (1992). A practice-centered model of organizational renewal through product innovation. *Strategic Management Journal, 13*, 77–92.

Eisenhardt, K. M., & Graebner, M. E. (2007). Theory building from cases: Opportunities and challenges. *Academy of Management Journal, 50*(1), 25–32.

Eskerod, P., & Riis, E. (2009a). Management models as value creators. *Project Management Journal, 40*(1) (Special Edition).

Eskerod, P., & Riis, E. (2009b). Value creation by building an intraorganizational common frame of reference concerning project management. *Project Management Journal, 40*(3), 6–13

Feller, I. (1981). Public sector innovation as "conspicuous consumption." *Policy Analysis, 7*, 1–20.

Fiol, C. M., & O'Connor, E. J. (2003). Waking up! Mindfulness in the face of bandwagons. *Academy of Management Review, 28*, 54–70.

Foucault, M. (1977). *Discipline and punish: The birth of the prison*. London, England: Penguin.

Foucault, M. (1978). *The will to knowledge: The history of sexuality* (vol. 1). London, England: Penguin.

Foucault, M. (1985). *The use of pleasure: The history of sexuality* (vol. 2). London, England: Penguin.

Foucault, M. (2002). Questions of method. In *Essential Works of Foucault 1954-1984* (pp. 223–238). London, England: Penguin.

Freitas, I. M. B. (2008). Sources of differences in the pattern of adoption of organizational and managerial innovations from early to late 1990s, in the UK. *Research Policy, 37(1)*, 131–148.

Giroux, H. (2006). It was such a handy term: Management fashions and pragmatic ambiguity. *Journal of Management Studies, 43(6)*, 1227–1260.

Grant, A., & Wall, T. (2008). The neglected science and art of quasi experimentation: Why to, when to, and how to advice for organizational researchers. *Organizational Research Methods, 12*(4), 653–686.

Gray, B., Stensaker, I., & Jensen, K. (2010). Call for papers: Studying change dynamics using qualitative methods. *The Journal of Applied Behavioral Science, 46*(1), 5–7.

Green, S. (2008). Discourse and fashion in supply chain management. In S. Pryke & H. Smyth (Eds.), *The management of complex projects—A relational approach.* Oxford, England: Blackwell.

Greenwood, R., & Hinings, C. R. (1996). Understanding radical organizational change: Brining together the old and new institutionalism. *Academy of Management Review, 21,* 1022–1054.

Greve, H. R., & Taylor, A. (2000). Innovations as catalysts for organizational change: Shifts in organizational cognition and search. *Administrative Science Quarterly, 45(1),* 54–80.

Gupta, A. K., Tesluk, P. E., & Taylor, M. S. (2007). Innovation at and across multiple levels of analysis. *Organization Science, 18(6),* 885–897.

Hackman, J. R., & Wageman, R. (1995). Total quality management: Empirical, conceptual and practical issues. *Administrative Sciences Quarterly, 40,* 309–342.

Hamel, G. (2006). The why, what, and how of management innovation. *Harvard Business Review, 84*(2), 72.

Hamel, G., & Breen, B. (2007). *The future of management.* Boston, MA: Harvard Business School Press.

Hill, S., & Wilkinson, A. (1995). In search of TQM. *Employee Relations, 17*(3), 8–25.

Hinings, C. R., & Greenwood, R. (1988). *The dynamics of strategic change.* Oxford, England: Blackwell.

Hobbs, B., Aubry, M., & Thuillier, D. (2008). The project management office as an organizational innovation. *International Journal of Project Management, 26(5),* 547–555.

Hofstede, G. (2001). *Culture's consequences: Comparing values, behaviors, institutions, and organizations across nations* (2nd ed.). Thousand Oaks, CA: SAGE.

Hofstede, G., Hofstede, G. J., Minkov, M. (2010). Cultures and organizations: Software of the mind (3rd ed.). New York: McGraw Hill.

Hurt, M., & Thomas, J. L. (2009). Building value through sustainable project management offices. *Project Management Journal, 40*(1) (Special Edition).

Kimberly, J. R., & Evanisko, M. J. (1981). Organizational innovation: The influence of individual, organizational and contextual factors on hospital adoption of technological and administrative innovations. *Academy of Management Journal, 24,* 689–713.

Knights, D., Noble, F., Vurdubakis, T., & Willmott, H. (2001). Chasing shadows: Control, virtuality, and the production of trust. *Organization Studies, 22*(2), 311–336.

Langley, A., Smallman, C., Tsoukas, H., & Van de Ven, A. H. (2010). Call for papers: Special research forum. Process studies of change in organization and management. *Academy of Management Journal.* Retrieved from http://journals. aomonline.org/amj/Research_Forums.html

Lechler, T. G., & Cohen, M. (2009). Exploring the role of steering committees in realizing value from project management. *Project Management Journal, 40*(1) (Special Edition).

McSweeney, B. (2002). Hofstede's model of national cultural differences and their consequences: A triumph of faith—a failure of analysis. Human Relations, 55(1), 89–118.

Mamman, B. A. (2009). From management innovation to management practise. The International Journal of Organizational Innovation, 2(2), 22–60.

March, J., & Olson, J. (1983). Organizing political life: What administrative reorganization tells us about government. The American Political Science Review 77(2), 281–296.

Marcus, A. A. (1988). Responses to externally induced innovation: Their effects on organizational performance, Strategic Management Journal, 9(4), 387–402.

Martinsuo, M., Hensman, N., Arto, K. A., & Kujalo, J. (2006). Project-based management as an organizational innovation: Drivers, changes, and benefits of adopting project-based management. Project Management Journal, 37(3), 87–97.

Mengel, T., Cowan-Sahadath, K. & Follert, F. (2009). The value of project management to organizations in Canada and Germany, or do values add value? Five Case Studies. Project Management Journal, 40(1) (Special Edition).

Meyer, A. D., Tsui, A. S., & Hinings, C. R. (1993). Configurational approaches to organizational analysis. Academy of Management Journal, 36, 1175–1195.

Miles, M. B., & Huberman, A. M. (1994). Qualitative data analysis. Thousand Oaks, CA: SAGE.

Morris, P. W. G., & Jamieson, A. (2005). Moving from corporate strategy to project strategy. Project Management Journal, 37(3), 62–74.

Myers, S., & Marquis, D. G. (1969). Successful industrial innovation: A study of factors underlying the innovation in selected firms. Paper No. NSF 69-17, National Science Foundation, Washington, DC.

Meyerson, D., & Martin, J. (1987). Cultural change: An integration of three different views. Journal of Management Studies, 24, 623–647.

Mullaly, M., & Thomas, J. L. (2009). Exploring the dynamics of value and fit: Insights from project management. Project Management Journal, 40(1) (Special Edition).

Nadler, D. A., & Tushman, M. L. (1989). Organizational frame bending: Principles for managing reorientation. The Academy of Management Executive, 3(3), 194–204.

Noon, M., Jenkins, S., & Lucio, M. M. (2000). Fads, techniques and control: The competing agendas of TPM and TECEX at the Royal Mail (UK). Journal of Management Studies, 37(4), 499–518.

O'Mahoney, J. (2007). The diffusion of management innovations: The possibilities and limitations of mimetics. Journal of Management Studies, 44(8), 1324–1348.

Obstfeld, D. (2005). Social networks, the teritus iungens orientation, and involvement in innovation. Administrative Science Quarterly, 50(1), 100–130.

Pettigrew, A. M. (2003). Innovative forms of organizing: Progress, performance, and process. In A. M. Pettigrew, R. Wittington, L. Melin, C. Sanchez-Runde, F. A. J. Van den Bosch, W. Ruigrok, & T. Numagami (Eds.), Innovative forms of organizing (pp. 331–351). London, England: SAGE.

Pettigrew, A. M., & Whipp, R. (1993). *Managing change for competitive success.* Oxford, England: Blackwell.

Plowman, D. A., Baker, L. T., Beck, T. E., Kulkarni, M., Solansky, S. T., & Travis, D. E. (2007). Radical change accidentally: The emergence and amplification of small change. *Academy of Management Journal, 50(3),* 515–543.

Quintane, E., Casselman, R. M., Reiche, B. S., & Nylund, P. (2011). Innovation as a knowledge-based outcome. *Journal of Knowledge Management, 15*(6), 928–947.

Pettigrew, A. M., Woodman, R. W., & Cameron, K. S. (2001). Studying organizational change and development: Challenges for future research. *The Academy of Management Journal, 44*(4), 697–713.

Rindova, V. P., & Petkova, A. P. (2007). When is a new thing a good thing? Technological change, product form design, and perceptions of value for product innovations. *Organization Science, 18*(2), 217–232.

Rogers, E. M. (1995). *Diffusion of innovations.* New York, NY: The Free Press.

Romanelli, E., & Tushman, M. L. (1994). Organizational transformation as punctuated equilibrium: An empirical test. *Academy of Management Journal, 37*(5), 1141–1166.

Schumpeter, J. A. (1934). The theory of economic development. Boston, MA: Harvard University Press.

Shenhar, A. J., & Dvir, D. (1996). Toward a typographical theory of project management. *Research Policy 25(4),* 607–632.

Shenhar, A. J., & Dvir, D. (2007). *Reinventing project management: The diamond approach to successful growth & innovation.* Boston, MA: Harvard Business School Press.

Srivannaboon, S., & Milosevic, D. Z. (2006). A two-way influence between business strategy and project management. *International Journal of Project Management, 24*(6), 493–505.

Stensaker, I., & Langley, A. (2010). Change management choices and change trajectories in a multidivisional firm. *British Journal of Management, 21*(1), 7–27.

Street, C. T., & Gallupe, R. B. (2009). A proposal for operationalizing the pace and scope of organizational change in management studies. *Organizational Research Methods, 12*(4), 720.

Swanson, E. B., & Ramiller, N. C. (2004). Innovating mindfully with information technology. *MIS Quarterly, 28*(4), 553–583.

Terziovski, M. (2010). Innovation practice and its performance implications in small and medium enterprises (SMEs) in the manufacturing sector: A resource-based view. *Strategic Management Journal, 31(8),* 892–902.

Thomas, J. (2006). Problematising project management. In D. Hodgson & S. Cicmil (Eds.), *Making projects critical* (pp. 90–110). Basingstoke, UK and New York, NY: Palgrave McMillan.

Thomas, J., Delisle, C. L., Jugdev, K., & Buckle, P. (2002). Selling project management to senior executives: The case for avoiding crisis sales. *Project Management Journal, 33*(2), 19–29.

Thomas, J., & George, S. (2012). Discussing value: Legitimation and multiple rationalities. Paper presented at the 6th Biannual Making Projects Critical conference in Manchester, England.

Thomas, J., & Mullaly, M. (2008). *Researching the value of project management.* Newtown Square, PA: PMI.

Thompson, P., & McHugh, D. (2002). *Work organisations* (3rd ed.). Basingstoke, UK: Palgrave.

Vaccaro, I. G., Jansen, J. J. P., Van Den Bosch, F. A. J., & Volberda, H. W. (2012). The moderating role of organizational size. *Journal of Management Studies, 49*(1), 28–51.

Van de Ven, A. H. (1986). Central problems in the management of innovation. *Management Science, 32*(5), 590–607.

Van de Ven, A. H., & Polley, D. (1992). Learning while innovating. *Organization Science, 3*(1), 92–116.

Van de Ven, A. H., & Poole, M. S. (2005). Alternative approaches for studying organizational change. *Organization Studies, 26(9),* 1377–1401.

Van Maanen, J. (1988). *Tales of the field.* Chicago, IL: University of Chicago Press.

Walker, R. M., Damanpour, F., & Devece, C. A. (2009). Management innovation and organizational performance: The mediating effect of performance management. *Journal of Public Administration Research, 21(2),* 367–386.

Weick, K. E., & Quinn, R. E. (1999). Organizational change and development. *American Review of Psychology, 50,* 361–386.

Weick, K. E., & Sutcliffe, K. M. (2001). *Managing the unexpected: Assuring high performance in an age of complexity.* San Francisco, CA: Jossey-Bass.

West, M. A. (2002). Sparkling fountains or stagnant ponds: An integrative model of creativity and innovation implementation in work groups. *Applied Psychology: An International Review, 51*(3) 355–424.

West, M. A., & Farr, J. L. (1990). Innovation at work. In M. A. West & J. L. Farr (Eds.), *Innovation and creativity at work: Psychological and organizational strategies.* Chichester, England: John Wiley.

Williams, T. (2007). *Post project reviews to gain effective lessons learned.* Newtown Square, PA: PMI.

Wood, T. Jr., & Caldas, M. (2002). Adopting imported managerial expertise in developing countries: The Brazilian experience. *The Academy of Management Executive, 16*(2), 18–32.

Wolfe, R. (1994). Organizational innovation: Review, critique and suggested research directions. *Journal of Management Studies, 31,* 405–431.

Yin, R. K. (2003). *Case study research* (3rd ed.). Thousand Oaks, CA: SAGE.

Zbaracki, M. J. (1998). The rhetoric and reality of total quality management. *Administrative Sciences Quarterly, 43,* 602–605.

Zhai, L., Xin, Y., & Cheng, C. (2009). Understanding the value of Project management from a stakeholders perspective: Case study of mega-project management. *Project Management Journal, 40*(1) (Special Edition).